MW00604973

True Synergy Works...Leading Within

Seven (7) Defining Principles of
Knowing Self to Birth Greatness!

Sharon Parker's Memoir Original
Parker Family
by aka "Sharon Lee"

"Destiny and Fulfillment: *Recovery-to-Discovery"*

© 2017 by Sharon Parker, ALL RIGHTS RESERVED

No part of this book may be used or reproduced by any means, graphic, electronic, online, video or mechanical to include photocopying, recording, taping or by any other information storage and retrieval system without the written permission of the author except in the case of brief quotations embodied in critical news articles and reviews.

Because of the dynamic nature of the Internet, any web addresses or links contained in this book may be used as permitted by the author through printing or providing links within electronic versions of this publication, unless otherwise stated by the author.

ISBN: 0692897356 USA

ISBN: 978-0692897355 International

Printed in the United States of America

"I Dedicate this book"—Sharon Parker

"To my Ancestors, what I learned from their history … and the world will learn from our future generations."

In memoriam: *"Rest in peace within God's arms."*

To my Great-Great Grandfather Benjamin Parker, Sr. and my Great Grandparents, Benjamin Parker, Jr. and Grace Parker; "You who started it all!"

To my Grandmother Hattie Parker; Mother Evelyn Parker; "Please know your hard work has not been in vain!"

To my loving sisters, Delores and Faith; to my youngest brother, Tony; to my little niece, Toshawna; "Shine your beacon of light upon us as you are now my Ancestors too."

In gratitude and love: *"Those who share this journey with me."*

To my Aunt Mary Elizabeth Parker-Willet, oldest living daughter of Hattie Parker; "For your love and commitment to your mother, family, and many friends."

To my children, grandchildren, God-daughter; "Reach for the stars and your dreams; remember your Ancestors!"

To my siblings, Clifton, Leo, Tracy, Kathy, Patty, Darlene, Bridgett, Lynn; "Remember what brought us back together in 2013-2014, three years after the passing of our mother.

And to my sweet, oldest Granddaughter, Shealah Cannon; "I choose you to take up the torch and keep the legacy alive when I am gone. Work hard and show unconditional love!

Shealah Cannon and Jordan Robinson (Visit at the White House in 2016)

Sharon, Little Known Facts

"It all started with three (3) Benjamin Parkers.

Yes, Benjamin Parker, Sr. born 1828;

Benjamin Parker, Jr. born 1865; and

Benjamin Parker, III born 1899."

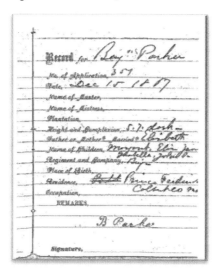

Benjamin Parker, Sr. born 1828. Sent via email by Lelia Bower, Calvert County Historical Society on 8-22-12. Note to Sharon from Lelia: **"The Freedmen's Bank account; Benjamin wasted NO time in opening that account. He was right there just about the time it started up!'** (*"The real dramatic thing for me, however, is to see his own handwriting there at the bottom of the page. Doesn't that make your arm hair stand up on end? It does me!"*—Sharon Parker)

 *Sharon's Timeline*

- ❖ **1963**, Sharon Parker was born: "The Civil Rights Baby who would ask God a question!"
- ❖ **1968**, Sharon Parker's life was saved by God, her two guardian angels: Hattie Parker and Valeria Hampton!
- ❖ **1979**, Sharon Lee's angel Tonique was born!
- ❖ **1980**, Sharon Lee's second angel Shawan was born!
- ❖ **1985**, Sharon Lee's third angel Wakeelah was born!
- ❖ **1987**, Sharon Lee's fourth angel Latifah was born!
- ❖ **1986**, Sharon Lee landed her first Government job with the Department of Agriculture!
- ❖ **1987**, Sharon Lee landed her second Government job with the Department of Housing and Urban Development!
- ❖ **1994-1998**, Sharon Lee attended the District of Columbia Community College and received her Computer Information System Science (CISS)!
- ❖ **1999-2001**, Sharon Lee attended Prince George's Community College for Business Management and Public Speaking!

❖ **2003**, Sharon Lee purchased a life-changing picture ("Beacon of Light from our Ancestors") from her now deceased Ancestor Shebah Aqeel!

"Sharon purchased the picture from Shebah Aqeel in 2003 at an art party Shebah held at her house in Brandywine, Maryland."

❖ **2007**, life-changing meeting with Shebah, Ty, and Sylvia which birthed the idea of Remembering Our Ancestors Synergistic Association (ROASA) Inc.!

❖ **2008**, Sharon Parker established the Remembering Our Ancestors Synergistic Association (ROASA, Inc.) in Maryland!

❖ **2010**, ROASA's Ancestral Sightings Program established (Showcase Our Elders)!

- ❖ **2010**, Sharon Parker's mother Evelyn M. Parker died! Sharon decides to write the "True Synergy Works" book for the first time!

- ❖ **2012**, ROASA's Youth Empowerment Series (RYES) pronounced "Rise"!

- ❖ **2012**, Sharon Parker becomes one of the Commissioners for the Maryland Commission on African-American History and Culture!

- ❖ **2013**, ROASA, Inc., hosted the first Annual Unconditional Love Retreat at the historical L'Enfant Plaza Hotel in SW Washington, DC!

- ❖ **2013**, Sharon Parker becomes American Mothers, Inc. – Mother of Achievement!

- ❖ **2014**, ROASA, Inc., hosted the 2nd Annual Unconditional Love Retreat in Maryland at the Zealia Center Room!

- ❖ **2015**, ROASA launches the Roadmap to Self-Workshop at the Department of Housing and Urban Develop for Robert C. Weaver--Blacks in Government on Rosa Parks birthday (February 4, 2017)!

- ❖ **2015**, Sharon Parker meets her real-life mentor, First Lady Michelle Obama!

- ❖ **2015**, ROASA, Inc., hosted the 3th Annual Unconditional Love Retreat in Washington, DC at the Resident Inn by the Capital!
- ❖ **2016**, Sharon Parker becomes President for Robert C. Weaver – Blacks in Government at HUD!
- ❖ **2016**, ROASA, Inc., hosted 4th Annual Unconditional Love Retreat in Maryland at the Serengeti Art Gallery!
- ❖ **2017**, ROASA's launches our Unconditional Love Café in Prince Frederick, Maryland on February 11th!
- ❖ **2017**, ROASA, Inc., will host our 5th Annual Leading WithIN Conference, formally called ROASA's Unconditional Love Retreat!
- ❖ **2017**, God released Sharon Parker's unsettledness within and gave her a Gift of her mother's Evelyn M. Parker's autopsy (May 17, 2017)!

Synergy

Synergy: "The interaction of elements that when combined produce a total effect that is greater … than the individual elements, contributions, etc."

–www.dictionary.com

Synergy: "Connect and network, remembering at least two things you have in common with the person to establish a 'meet-and-greet' based on the present to create a meaningful, lasting relationship that grows and becomes **MORE** with evolving history."

—Sharon Parker

Synergy: "When the sum of the parts that make up a whole is immeasurably larger than equal to the parts combined."

—D.A. Bowman Davisson, Publications Authorization Officer, Department of the Army 1983-1989

"True Synergy Works, not merely by definition, but rather by the actions created by the words."

—Sharon Parker and D. A. Bowman, 2017

Remembering Our Ancestors Synergistic

Association, Inc.
<u>Seven (7) Principles of Knowing Self to Birth Greatness!</u>

<u>www.roasalives.org</u>   <u>www.leadingwithin.org</u>

- ❖ Principal 1: Know who's leading you!
- ❖ Principal 2: Be lead-able!
- ❖ Principal 3: Know where you came from (family)!
- ❖ Principal 4: Position yourself for greatness!
- ❖ Principal 5: Study your past to change the future!
- ❖ Principal 6: Assure success for the next generation!
- ❖ Principal 7: Map a pathway of success to yield personal, professional, spiritual, educational, and economical success in all your endeavors!

Table of Contents

Table of Contents (continued)

 # Foreword

"I have been touched by the gracious hand of God!"

—Sharon Parker

His nimble fingers pointed the direction that *He* wanted me to take for my life when I was five years old. Even though in my young innocence I had asked God a searching question, I didn't follow His direction. In fact, I denied the path He had predestined for me by denying my own memories. This was never a conscious decision on my part.

But how was I to know that my future was linked to my past? A past I had hidden from everyone, and everyone had hidden from me. Maybe, they had hidden it from themselves as well.

I placed all the *"auspicious occurrences"* concerning my family and my childhood, the good and the bad, in a big, strong box; then, I sealed it shut … very tightly. I put it out of sight, out of mind.

I planned to rise above my background—to succeed in life in spite of all that had happened to the sad, quiet little girl that I was back then, when I thought of myself as only an *"omission."*

Many decades later, I realized that "all the past; all our history" is linked to the future. If we don't know our history, we can't fulfill our destiny.

I didn't realize that I had to claim my past to transform my life from *"omission to commission."* The past, you see, was the foundation for the future. It had been God's plan for me all along … if I had but opened my eyes to see His hand guiding me.

I am Sharon Parker, aka little five-year-old Sharon Lee. I've been instrumental in helping disadvantaged families and communities for over 30 years as a public servant for the Federal Government. I had always known my true purpose was to give back and to lend a helping hand. But that wasn't ALL I was supposed to do!

Now I realize that even though God singled me out to search for these truths, I was to find them and keep finding them to embrace and give of them to everyone. For no one can be whole and *"synergistic"* without all the pieces of the whole; the pieces that become more (I've found so much more!) than the sum of the individual parts. That is how *"True Synergy Works!"*

The Aspen Grove—roots depend on other roots to grow -"True Synergy Works"

We evolve closer to the epiphany of humankind by understanding where we have come from on the journey of life in relation to other paths different from our own. We become more completely "whole" when we see all the perspectives, perceptions, and viewpoints ... every race, every color, every ethnicity, every religion, EVERYONE!

The synergy of family, community, society, and the entire world is built brick-upon-brick, block-by-block, and most importantly, sealed boxes are ripped open; the contents spilling forth to synergize with the contents of all the other sealed boxes, hidden for so long, which will be torn asunder. But share them delicately, reverently, respectfully.

After I was led by the grace of God to grasp my heritage and unleash my repressed memories, I established "Remembering Our Ancestors Synergistic Association, Inc." www.roasalives.org which is a not-for-profit organization that teaches we are designed in our Maker's image to reach out and capture, firmly embrace as our own, and lovingly share with young people, the future generations, the strength and wisdom of our elders—their joys and triumphs as well as their struggles and defeats. We learn invaluable truths from all aspects of our histories, the good and the bad, the lessons-learned.

I may have had to learn the hard way, but much can be said of stubbornness that sustains and encourages. Once we learn a hard lesson, of course, we never forget it. But more than that, it enlivens our focus and takes off on a well-defined path of its own, following the direction of the Divine. Synergy is at work here, you see, in abundance!

With the 5th anniversary of my ROASA retreat, now a Conference (*there's that auspicious number 5 again"*) I feel the time is right to share my story—***"Sharon Parker's Memoir Original Parker Family by aka Sharon Lee"***— from the shy, quiet little girl who feared to ask a question of the Almighty to the woman introvert who had to break out of her shell and her comfort zone to help all children and families I touch on this journey of discovery and growth.

"Just as God reached out to take me by the hand!"

—Sharon Parker, author

 *Preface*

by Charles Cary, National Trainer, Speaker, Author, Coach

Let me just say that Sharon Parker is not afraid of hard work...even when she doesn't have to work hard, she doesn't mind. She has worked for or volunteered for several national organizations as well as been a Commissioner for the Maryland Commission of African-American History and Culture, which most recently developed a relationship with the National African-American Museum of African History.

The content of this book is a direct reflection of how dialed-in she is to history and her own story. Her family's story is interwoven into history, just as so many other families are. The difference is that she's doing the work to bring that story into the marvelous light.

When we think about our lives and where we come from, there is so much that has happened. However, when you find yourself remembering situations and incidents here and there...trust me, it's for a reason. Many of those situations are silent reminders of significant occurrences in your life and you should never take them lightly. You see that we are all here for a reason, and it's up to you to find that reason and tap into it.

A full commitment to yourself should never be too much to ask for. Sharon has realized in flashes and in memories what she's been put here to do, and **she has signed on to empower and encourage young people all over about how significant their lives can be if they know their own self!** The African-American Experience has been talked about, relived, sensationalized, monetized and none of it has helped us as much as we can potentially help ourselves.

She's pulled out all the stops through various programs that her organization offers to become a National Connector and a Game Changer! Whether it's annual events, youth events, senior events or vision boards...She is in it for the long haul!

Sharon has been preparing for the debut of this book for quite some time, and I think you will be glad to share in this experience with her. Whether you know Sharon from a professional or a social engagement, there's always a certain part of her that is analyzing and preparing for the next big thing...and my friends, trust me, when I tell you *THIS IS IT!* **"True Synergy Works!"**

Introduction

"Mom, you have been chosen to tell our family's story ...
with all that you have shared with me over the years.
You MUST write a book about your experiences ...
and share those experiences because they happened
to you for a reason!"

—Tonique Parker, Sharon's oldest daughter

Mother and Daughter Sharon Parker (left); Tonique Parker (right)

Okay, my darling daughter, here is the story we've talked about for your whole life, slipping out of the nooks and crannies of my forgotten memories in tiny fragments when I least expected; confusing me, surprising me, but thankfully challenging me.

You were my guiding light, who listened and questioned, cajoling me; sometimes even arguing with me, but always … always loving me as I loved you.

Here is the book of our roots, our family's history, that we discussed long into the night, early on hurried mornings, through quiet afternoons, and even during turbulent times in our lives. Pieces we put together like a jigsaw puzzle, juggled up in the air, many times dropping on the ground in misunderstanding, but clarity would eventually break through and *auspiciously occur;* then, we would look at each other in silence and wonder what it all meant and why?

Here finally is the tale of a little girl named Sharon Lee, who could not stop running from her destiny, but it is so much more than that, and you know it!

I will tell my story through the eyes of a five-year-old child, who is now an aspiring adult, but still that scared, timid child within; a part of 'Sharon Lee' will remain in my heart and soul forever, as it should be.

We must never forget where we came from, who our Ancestors are, and what our history tells us about the future. We must recognize and accept the journey we were placed upon this earth to transverse; the pathway God chose for me that I have denied and hidden for over 40 years, which you, dear daughter, have aided me in accessing.

This is the story of The Original Parker Family of Adelina Road, and it must be shared with the world. Now, I truly understand that I have been chosen to share an empowering story on an emotional journey of remembrance, love, dislike, fear, and uncertainty about a near-forgotten legacy. It would have been a tragedy for this story to have been lost.

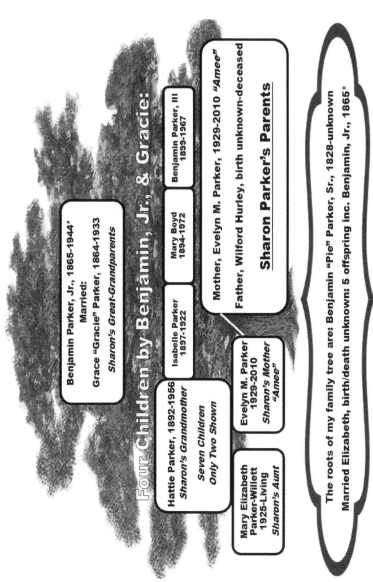

Four Children by Benjamin, Jr., & Gracie:

Benjamin Parker, Jr., 1865-1944*
Married:
Grace "Gracie" Parker, 1864-1933
Sharon's Great-Grandparents

Benjamin Parker, III
1899-1967

Mary Boyd
1894-1972

Isabelle Parker
1897-1922

Hattie Parker, 1892-1956
Sharon's Grandmother

*Seven Children
Only Two Shown*

Mary Elizabeth
Parker-Willett
1925-Living
Sharon's Aunt

Evelyn M. Parker
1929-2010
*Sharon's Mother
"Amee"*

Mother, Evelyn M. Parker, 1929-2010 *"Amee"*
Father, Wilford Hurley, birth unknown-deceased

Sharon Parker's Parents

The roots of my family tree are: Benjamin "Pie" Parker, Sr., 1828-unknown
Married Elizabeth, birth/death unknown: 5 offspring inc. Benjamin, Jr., 1865*

SHARON PARKER'S FAMILY TREE

Sharon Lee, the little girl who could not stop running

Section I

"Sharon Lee"

Chapter One

A Little Girl Caught in the Shadows

"This book is written for every five-year-old girl that lives within a grown woman ... a woman who has discovered her true purpose through recovery, auspicious occurrences, and the relentless power of God."

—Sharon Parker

The one memory that has been with me for my whole life was like a quick, clipped edit from a movie scene. I was a character called *"Sharon Lee,"* a name used by my family during my childhood; a name that became a ghost haunting my mind for many, many years. I could see it, hear it, almost touch it, but then it would become lost in the shadows like the rest of my memories. I didn't seem to notice and as I got older, I didn't care. The shadows and darkness were just a part of my life.

"The Church Where the Questions Was Ask!"

The year was 1968. I was playing in a field on the church grounds of the Carroll Western Church in my hometown. I was alone, but I preferred quiet and solitude. I had always felt safe there, just as I was safe in the light of God when we attended services. Church was the only place where the shadows did not dim the light into total darkness, but I was beginning to sense a heaviness in the grownups around me. I still saw their hope, light, and love, but at this tender age I didn't know the world was changing for all of us tucked away in our rural southern town. Nor did I know the history from which we had been formed.

Unaware of all the fear, tears, and turmoil in the United States of America in 1968, I stopped playing and asked aloud, *"God, why is it that blacks are hated by whites and why do we struggle so much?"*

I don't know where the question came from or why I asked it. I waited, expecting an answer. When I didn't get one, I went back to playing in this field where I had always felt so comfortable.

It wouldn't be until decades later that I would receive an answer to my question. I would have to work very hard for it, investing much time and energy, but the rewards would be bountiful beyond my wildest imagination! This has been a lifelong test of my faith and beliefs, for even at five years old I knew I was placed upon this earth to help others, as perhaps I had not been helped myself.

I had to find out on my own that these *auspicious occurrences* would continue to happen to me as signs and gifts from *Him* in dreams and clues that I didn't understand. But God had chosen *me*—no matter how far I ran away or how long I waited—*He* had a plan for me.

My first *auspicious occurrence,* my first memory? A mere child, a baby in many ways, I didn't realize that across the street from where I was playing in the churchyard was where my family home had once stood, the Benjamin and Grace Parker, Jr. Estate—my great-grandparents—44 acres on Adelina Road where I was born in 1963 in a little town called Prince Frederick, Maryland.

I remembered none of this.

"A child born under oppression has all the elements of servility in its constitution."

—Martin Delany

I may not have been born in slavery, but in my formative years I felt captive in a vicious cycle that eroded my sense of self and family to the point of oppression and omission, unconsciously blocking my memories to stop the pain.

"It is impossible to pretend that you are not heir to, and therefore, however inadequately or unwillingly, responsible to, and for, the time and place that gave you life—without becoming, at very best, a dangerously disoriented human being."

—James Baldwin

Yes, I was *"disoriented"* and disconnected, but by my own *subconscious* choice and circumstances beyond my control. Years later, my mother would tell me that something else happened at an early age which was completely erased from my mind, along with all I had known prior to and after the incident. This pattern of blacking out my memories would continue long into the future.

I had been extremely traumatized when my mother, myself, and seven siblings moved out of our ancestral home due to a fire in the kitchen of the Parker Estate. Our family was separated and moved to different family members' and friends' homes until the kitchen could be repaired … or so we thought.

August 28, 1963: "I Have a Dream...!"

—Dr. Martin Luther King, Jr.

This book, which goes back to 1968 when I was five years old, is part autobiography and part history. I will share little known facts of historical significance that occurred in America that includes my African-American heritage.

1963 Little Known Fact: The March on Washington Brings 250,000 to Demonstrate for Civil Rights, King Makes His Famous, "I Have a Dream" speech.

Source: *Atlas of African-American History ... revised by James Ciment*

Auspiciously, I was born in 1963 when the Civil Rights Movement was being discussed, planned, and later executed. A late baby boomer, I came into this world on May 23, 1963, in the deep country of Calvert County, Maryland. Well, maybe not so deep since Calvert County is only about an hour's drive from Washington, D.C., where the famous "March" took place, but it seemed to me growing up I was stuck in the deep south and I wanted to get as far away from this environment as possible.

1968 Little Known Fact: Martin Luther King, Jr. was assassinated. On April 4, 1968, the world was stunned and saddened by the news that the civil rights activist and Nobel

Peace Prize winner Martin Luther King, Jr. had been shot and killed on the balcony of a motel in Memphis, TN.

Source: *Atlas of African-American History ... revised edition by James Ciment*

Auspiciously, my singular, significant memory of 1968, which carried me through shadowed years of denial and escape, corresponds with the death of the greatest Civil Rights Leader of the 20th Century. I was totally removed and blind to this devastating historical fact. Yet, history caught up with me and set me on a path to build synergy in my own community. This played right into God's Hand for me to research my own family's legacy and return home.

"This book will describe people, black and white, who touched my life and gave me encouragement and enlightenment to help me understand the racial status quo in America today. I can't believe I'm saying 'racial status quo' in 2017 ... history has repeated itself 50 years later. It is my hope that readers will be left with words like captivated, encouraged, enlightened, inspired, and empowered."

—Sharon Parker

Chapter Two

The History of Prince Frederick, MD

"A people without the knowledge of their past history, origin, and culture is like a tree without roots."

—Marcus Garvey

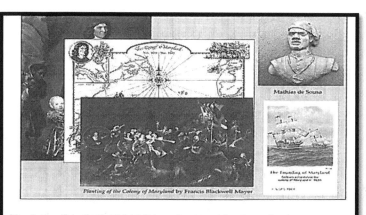

Planting of the Colony of Maryland by Francis Blackwell Mayer

Mathias de Sousa

The Founding of Maryland

Review of early So Md history in one minute or less:

The Maryland colony was founded in 1634. The portrait of Cecilius Calvert, Lord Baltimore, shows a young, presumably African servant in the shadows behind him. People of color were reported on the first ship that sailed to settle the colony: Mathias de Sousa sailed on the Ark in 1634. De Sousa was an indentured servant of the Jesuits,(Father Andrew White, de Sousa's Jesuit "master" is circled in red in the Mayer painting) and served a period of four years, before he was freed. He voted in the legislative body after that. De Sousa is an ambiguous historical character in that his identity, other than his name and social status, is unknown. His name his Portuguese, he may have been African by birth.

The first people described as slaves arrived in 1644, according to Roland McConnell in <u>350 years, a Chronology of the Afro-Americans in Maryland.</u>

Image from the Calvert County Zoning and Planning, Archaeologist, Kirsdi Uunlla.

I was so proud of my Ancestors when I learned that Prince Frederick, a small farming community in southern Maryland, was one of the first African-American townships in Colonial America, dating back to the early 17th century. It is believed to have been named for British King George II's son Frederick, the Prince of Wales, who reigned during the early decades of the African-American Colony, which would later become Calvert County.[1]

Originally settled by predominantly slaves with few white masters, their families, and freed slaves referred to as "freemen of color," the people of my roots and their descendants had to legally fight to become incorporated into a city, and fight they did for over two centuries!

Prince Frederick, however, was recognized as the county seat of Calvert County, Maryland, since 1722. In this year, officials selected Williams's Old Field, a plot of vacant farmland, upon which to build the county courthouse. This courthouse was not completed until 1732, a full decade later.

In the 1800s, Prince Frederick was burned to the ground ... *twice!* I shudder when I try to imagine the horrific tragedy my forefathers and mothers had to endure as everything they

[1] Calvert County was established in 1654, Calvert County Historical Society.

had fought and worked so hard for was suddenly gone in a matter of hours or days. They watched as their rich fields of crops, where they'd shed blood, sweat, and tears from sunup to sundown, rose up in flames. And how could they ever recover from the pain of death and injury to family members, relatives, and friends? And yet, they continued and rebuilt.

Since my childhood was traumatized and my family separated by a small fire, I felt I could relate in an extremely miniscule way. I was humbled to tears when I realized how I had been blessed that all my family members had survived, but it did register in my mind that the fear, loss, and devastation of fire was mired in the very soil under my feet. Another auspicious occurrence? Perhaps … perhaps …

The first fire was during the War of 1812. It was June of 1814 and Commodore Joshua Barney sought refuge for the Chesapeake Bay Flotilla at St. Leonard's Creek, just a few miles from Prince Frederick. British Admiral Sir Alexander Cochrane burned Barney's fleet, resulting in much of the town and farmlands outside of Prince Frederick to be destroyed by fire.

The second fire in 1882[2] was of unknown origin, but was massive in destruction, burning down the entire town including the original courthouse.[3] A new courthouse was erected at the same location, and this building still houses Calvert County's official government offices.

My life seems so trivial in comparison—*little shy, quiet Sharon Lee*—yet this early history is an integral, emotional part of me, my Ancestors, and our future generations to come. We must experience the past to honor our Ancestors and create a brighter, more loving, blessed future!

"Located just south of Washington, D.C.,
Calvert County's African-American community
can be traced back to the county's beginning
in the 17th century."

—William A. "Billy" Poe

Source: *Images of America, African Americans of Calvert County, Arcadia Press ©2008*

[2]Rumor was, *"A child caused the fire; it may have been intentionally set; or it may have been an accident. It was a windy day and the fire spread fast and burned a lot of homes in Prince Frederick."* Calvert County Historical Society.

[3]The courthouse was burnt down and deeds, birth records, marriage records were lost. The "Parkers" who lived in District 2 (African-Americans) on Adelina Road and Lusby, Maryland, homes were not impacted by the fire in 1882. Some very important court deed records were needed as it showed how much land Sharon Parker's great-grandparents owned ... approximately 44 acres. The "Parkers" who lived in District 1 were in Prince Frederick "city limits" and it was believed this was a Caucasian family, Calvert County Historical Society.

"From a time when Calvert County's black population grew to approximately 60 percent of the populace, to its present-day residents representing the national average of 12 percent, Calvert's African-Americans have attempted to hold onto many of their rich cultural traditions."

—William A. "Billy" Poe

Source: *Images of America, African Americans of Calvert County, Arcadia Press ©2008*

As history evolved around and through Prince Frederick, my small hometown became a unique African-American community, especially on Adelina Road where African-Americans once owned the majority of large, prosperous farms. At the time, this was unheard of in the United States of America.

In the 1960s, Albert Irvin Cassell, an influential architect from Washington, D.C., planned to develop 520 acres as a Summer Resort for African-Americans to be called Chesapeake Heights on the Bay. Some headway was made on this project with new roads and a few homes, but was halted upon Cassell's death in 1969.

From the 1970s through the end of the century, a major shift would occur in the demographics of Prince Frederick for both blacks and whites with the regulation and limitation placed on tobacco farming in Maryland. Land owners would be forced to sell their once equitable cropland for pennies on the dollar. Black owners were offered much less for their properties than white owners. African-Americans were reduced to sharecroppers, working day and night at multiple jobs just to keep their families fed.

This is the Prince Frederick that existed when I was born in 1963 and remembered as a five-year-old child in 1968. Our family was struggling long before the fire in the kitchen of our home. There was just no money to repair the damages.

The racial discrimination that was rampant in America from the Emancipation Proclamation in the mid-1800s to the desegregation and civil rights laws of the 1950s, 60s, and 70s left its ugly mark on our hometown as well. In the 1930s and 40s, black children only went to the 7th grade. The first teachers, predominantly white, were brought in from Hampton, Virginia, starting in 1942 because few black teachers existed, having had no chance for higher education. Up through 1960, an African-American could not legally enter a public library. When African-Americans were finally allowed a high school education, there were two separate, segregated high schools.

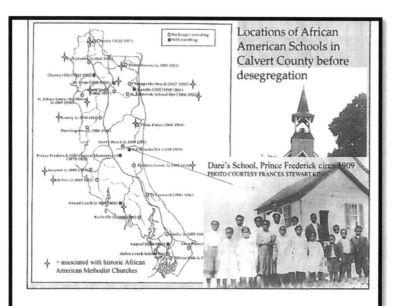

Locations of African American Schools in Calvert County before desegregation

Dare's School, Prince Frederick circa 1909
PHOTO COURTESY FRANCES STEWART KIN...

Education is a useful thread to help understand how African American communities worked before desegregation, which did not take place in Calvert County until the 1966-67 school year. The early schools were established by the communities themselves, usually utilizing church buildings. When the county was forced to extend public education to African American children, the Board of Ed purchased the community school buildings and incorporated them into the public school system. The schools were typically one-room structures and grades 1 through 7 were instructed together in the same room—the older students would assist the younger ones. As in the white schools, one-room school teachers played all roles in the schools from instructor to administrator to custodian. The teachers were also advocates for the children, making do with little—the schools were equipped with castoffs from the white schools. The teachers were often resourceful and some were activists.

For more information, see *Persistence, Perseverance and Progress: History of African American Schools in Calvert County, Maryland, 1865-1965* by Richlyn F. Goddard, Calvert County Government, 1996. You can now visit the Old Wallville School in Prince Frederick—and will, as the last stop on our tour today.

Image from the Calvert County Zoning and Planning, Archaeologist, Kirsdi Uunlla.

One glowing victory for African-American education in Prince Frederick was in 1937 Harriet R. Brown brought a lawsuit against the Board of Education, Calvert County, Maryland, for equal pay of white and black female teachers. Thurgood Marshall, prior to becoming a Supreme Court Justice, litigated and won this case for Harriet R. Brown.

Regardless, African-American parents wanted their children to move away from Prince Frederick to pursue higher education and better employment opportunities. All of this history, which was never taught even when I attended public school in Prince Frederick up through 1982, had totally altered this once thriving African-American community. I can remember that during my high school years, I too only wanted to graduate so I could leave Prince Frederick and attend college.

Looking back on my life, I realize that growing up in Prince Frederick, Maryland, has had a significant impact upon my soul's journey. Prince Frederick's African-American heritage dwindled into obscurity just as my repressed memories shadowed God's true purpose and pathway for my future. It would take many years, tears, and fears for me to realize that my home, my family, and my Ancestors were as much as part of me as their blood that runs in my veins.

"We only know our stories if we tell our story."

—Lydia Mason Gladden, Prince Frederick, MD
Daughter of William H. and Mary Mason
Cousin to the Parker Family

I gave much thought about whether to include Prince Frederick's tangled history as part of my personal memoir. Although it is only about an hour's drive from Washington, D.C., to a five-year-old, it was a world away.

"Your world is as big as you make it!"

—Georgia Douglas Johnson

Chapter Three

The House That Lit Up the Night!

"It was a large, yellow house with a red roof and a porch all the way around it. There was an apple orchard in the front and peach trees in the back. I had to pass that house every day on my way to school. It was the most beautiful house I'd ever seen, especially at night..."

—Johnny Brooks, *"The Rod Father"*

Even though my memoir has been silent, secretly living and breathing inside of me for over 50 years since the time of my birth, and The Original Parker Family story now spans five generations - *I do seem to attract that auspicious number 5; don't I?* - this book has only been in the making for a little over six years since 2010. Granted, a rather lengthy time.

Sharon Parker and Johnny "The Rod Rather Brooks

Some of those years, however, it was merely a dream. Something I felt I *should do,* but I wasn't entirely sure why because there was still much of my family history that I didn't know. *But good things come to those who* wait, as we all know, for not all the auspicious occurrences had yet been revealed.

It wasn't until recently that I found the pathway that would bring it all together. It took a lot of soul-searching, self-discovery, but mostly the power of prayer. *Ask and ye shall receive* ... five-year-old Sharon Lee's answers came in a torrent, once the floodgates of my darkened memories were torn open, but it could only happen with the blessings of God and the wonderful people He put in my path to help me.

On November 15, 2016, I was blessed to be granted an interview with a living legend named Johnny Brooks. Surprisingly—*another auspicious occurrence, of course*—we had both grown up on Adelina Road, and our lives would align after *five* decades to take us on an emotional road trip of memories, tragedies, failures, unbelievable gifts, and glorified blessings. I want to take *YOU* on that trip with me!

It is said that when you finally discover your purpose in life, your destiny, you must reconnect with the past that shaped you into the person that you have become. In my case, it was even more imperative because connecting with my past meant remembering my past, which for many decades I was reluctant to do. But who knew that thirteen years before I was born that sixteen-year-old Johnny Brooks would leave Adelina Road to follow his destiny as well? It was in 1950:

"I got tired of working on the farm [the Dukes and Hanes] *and growing tobacco ... I wanted to use my hands for the things I love and that's building antique cars."*

—Johnny Brooks

When Johnny Brooks left Adelina, he went to Baltimore, Maryland, going to work for Fox Ford on July 5, 1950. Later, he went to New York City, and when I talked to him at his home where he now resides back in Prince Frederick, it was filled with so many trophies, awards, and special recognition for his "hot rods" and antique street cars, the house was overflowing with them. I couldn't believe my eyes! But the best for me was yet to come when 81-year-old Johnny Brooks told me that he'd known the Parker Family and remembered the Estate in vivid detail ... *in living color*, so to speak.

At the time when Johnny walked to school, there was no electricity on Adelina Road, but my Great-Grandfather Benjamin, Jr. had *"some kind of generator, called compound light which lit up all day and all night. At night, you could see that house shining all through Adelina ... for miles and miles. It was the most beautiful thing I'd ever seen..."*

I was eight years old when Mr. Brooks returned with his family to Adelina Road. Forty-five years later, I would interview him to recognize his amazing achievements for Black History Month the following February.

Do the math, I was 8 years old when he returned *home*, and I started my non-profit organization ROASA, "Remembering Our Ancestors Synergistic Association, Inc." in 2008 at the age of 45, the exact number of years until we met again under auspicious circumstances, for there was something even more important pertaining to me about to occur...

Mr. Brooks had been 16 when he left the fields of Adelina. He reminded me—little did he know I didn't really remember—that I rode with his 16-year-old son to high school because *he* had a car. We were buddies who laughed and joked about everything, just as all teenagers do.

Mr. Brooks also told me that everyone at school always knew, even as a child, that I would grow up to be an entrepreneur because I sold candy at church as well as in the community and evidently, I was pretty successful at it, driving a hard bargain and making sure I was paid.

With this long-overdue reunion, Mr. Brooks gave me the history lesson that would fill in the gaps and complete my memoir. The historical significance in the timing of my life during the Civil Rights era and the 21st century was an act of God. So much more than just an auspicious occurrence to get my attention!

Thank you, Johnny Brooks, for bringing the things back to light that I'd hidden in the shadows of my mind or willingly forgotten. I could see and understand my past for the first time so that I could finally accept it in the pure light of God.

Using Johnny Brooks's words...

"...like the lone house on Adelina Road, the Parker Home, that lit up the pitch-black of night..."

Chapter Four

Sharon Lee ... Lost and Forgotten

*"There comes a time when one in the family
is chosen to continue the work that those
in the spiritual realm can no longer finish."*

—Anonymous saying

Upon reflection as I put pen to paper, metaphorically, I wonder if I was chosen by God to find out the true legacy of our family by asking my yearning question at the age of five? What if I hadn't done that?

Now that I have come full circle and pieced the story together, ready to share it with family and the world, I am curious why that memory was the only one I recalled for many years; why even in my darkest hours I never forgot the way I felt in 1968: *"lost, forgotten, and unwanted little Sharon Lee."* Shouldn't I have chosen to erase this memory?

I have come up with two conclusions on this nagging thought which I believe are relative and true. It isn't an option of one or the other, but rather both working in tandem:

1. Energy in the spiritual universe, from God the Almighty, is very powerful, indeed, and don't I know it! Even though I wasn't aware of the Civil Rights issues in 1963 through 1968 with the death of Dr. Martin Luther King, Jr., somehow my sensitivity and innocence could *feel* the hatred and discrimination across America as well as in my own community.

2. Five years old is an extremely impressionable age. You're not a baby or toddler anymore, but you're not really a *"big girl"* yet either. It's a time when your first memories become clear and set in your mind. Trauma, such as what took place in my life, left a strong lasting impression.

After the fire in the kitchen, which at five years old I knew nothing about, nor did I remember the fire, the house, or the plot of land across from the church. My memories just seemed to turn off in my head. I was confused why the family had been separated, and I was terrified by not being with my mother, brothers and sisters. The fear in my mind was that it had been all my fault—*Had I been bad and forced to leave my siblings?* My questions no matter what age I was as a grew up always were the pleading, tearful sobs of a five-year-old. I was lost, forgotten, lonely, and no longer part of the family.

I was placed in a dilapidated house with friends of the family, but I didn't really know them or didn't remember them; I'm not sure which.

There was no electricity or running water. No bathrooms or necessary rooms, as the ladies called them back then, like I was used to. The front yard was filled with junky cars that didn't work. It reminded me of the junkyard house on the TV show, "Stanford and Son." Only it wasn't funny at all!

My mind was filled with questions: *"Where am I? Where did my brothers and sisters go? Were they living with other people too or had they all died in the fire? Where was my mother? Why was I sent to this run-down, rickety house?* **What had I done wrong?"**

I couldn't make any sense out of what was going on. I was scared, traumatized, and always searching for answers that never came. It seemed like I lived this way for years. Recently, in 2016, my older brother Leo told me during Thanksgiving Day dinner that it had only been for a few months, but it was like an eternity in the fires of damnation to my battered and scarred recollections. It was no wonder that I chose to block out some of these dark, dreary, lonely days and nights.

I did remember reuniting with my mother and siblings when we moved into an old, cramped trailer that belonged to one of my cousins. I didn't care that it was small and crowded because we were all back together, but we weren't there for long. My mother didn't want to stay in this trailer. At the time, I didn't know why. She rented an old shack owned by the African-American "White" (their last name) family, but we didn't stay there long either. This was where my little brother Tony died. I remember he was no longer going to be with us, that he had gone to heaven, but I was too little or too confused to remember the details.

After Tony's death, we moved into a three-room shack, all 9-10 of us. It was unclear to me how many of us lived in this small, run-down hut owned by the Henson family. There would be a sister, Lynn, born after we became poor vagabonds, but I stayed there until I started running away from home when I was twelve years old, which I continued to do on numerous occasions. I didn't finally stop running until after I left Prince Frederick.

"My Mantra was, Run Sharon Run!"

—Sharon Parker

The first time I ran away, I went down Adelina Road, which is all I had ever known, just a few houses from where we were staying, and my brother quickly found me and brought me home.

In 1975, at the youthful age of 12, a pre-teen, I started running away in earnest. I stayed with one of my neighborhood friends, the Gross/Johnson family who lived at the very end of Adelina Road on the Dukes farm. I was sick and tired of living in a three-room shack, having to answer not only to my mother but my older siblings too. I spent the whole summer with this family, and it was like a breath of fresh air and a taste of freedom.

After I left the Gross/Johnson family home, I went to stay with my best friend, Sandra Buck, who lived in Lusby, Maryland. I was now 13 years of age. I spent two summers with the Bucks and loved every minute of it! I had many "first experiences" at the Buck family home: my very first job; my first boyfriend; my first *"company"—ladies, you know what I mean*—and unfortunately, my first heartbreak.

Some people may have said back then or even be thinking it as you read my story: *"Only 12 or 13 years old? That's way too young for a little girl to be on her own, away from home. Where were your mother and father or your older brothers and sisters?"* But to me, I felt like I'd never really had *"a home"* after we left the Parker Ancestral Estate, which I didn't even remember.

It didn't seem like it was very long at all after we left the beautiful, large Parker house that it was demolished, knocked down to the ground and erased from my heart and mind; my memories totally jumbled and hidden in shadows. I didn't know exactly when this destruction happened, and I certainly didn't know why!

After living with the Bucks, I moved in with the Dawkins family. It was around 1979 and I was starting high school, the 9th grade. One of the Dawkins's boys was just starting high school too. The Dawkins had just moved to Calvert County from District Heights, Maryland. I imagined that it was so far away in a big city near the District of Columbia. It sounded like another world!

The girls in my 9th grade class were all excited that one of the Dawkins's boys was a popular football player at Calvert High—*Weren't all football players popular and adored in high school?* I thought I was the luckiest girl in school when I fell *in love* with the football player nicknamed Casanova. Now, I'm sure he was called that for a reason, but I was just a silly high school kid then and thought he was *in love* with me as well.

Casanova was proud of his nickname, carrying it on his sleeve as he courted the hallways of Calvert High, watching and flirting with every young girl, probably making them feel like he cared about them too.

The Dawkins family only lived in Calvert County for a short time, but I was hooked on Casanova and the fast, exciting life he had shown me. They moved back to District Heights, Maryland, and guess who went along with them? It was the first time I had ever ventured beyond Prince Frederick in Calvert County, and I couldn't wait to go! Actually, it was just in the next county over, only a 45-minute drive, but I felt like I was living in New York City! I'd left the deep south behind.

"He who starts behind in the great race of life must forever remain behind or run faster than the man in front."

—Benjamin E. Mays

# Chapter Five

My Mother's Story, the Parker Estate

"There's an old saying that when you go home,
your family will take you in and care for you,
but what if there isn't a home to go back to?"

—Sharon Parker, thinking of her mother

My mother, Evelyn M. Parker, was forced to make some hard decisions in 1968, when I was the next to the youngest of the children living with her on the Parker Estate, age 5. She either had to go back to the family home after the fire where there was no kitchen in which to cook for her children or find some place to rent until the kitchen could be restored.

There may have been additional damage to the walls and windows of the house which would have caused ventilation, heating, and electrical problems. It wasn't known whether the structure of the large house was safe or not. I was too young to know or remember if anyone ever checked out the house or not. In fact, I didn't even remember seeing the large Estate at all until I saw of picture of it after I had reached adulthood.

Benjamin and Grace Parker, Jr. Estate, Oldest Child was Hattie Parker. Above three of Hattie's children: Catherine Harris (left), Mary Elizabeth Willett (right), and my mother, Evelyn M. Parker (middle bottom).

As I have mentioned before, we never went back to the Parker Estate, and this was the beginning of another sad tale I must tell in the memoir of The Original Parker Family about how my Grandmother Hattie Parker's legacy was almost lost. Not going back to the house also started my disconnection to the family and the repression of my childhood memories.

The women of the Parker family, thankfully, are strong women who never gave up or gave in during hard times. Our faith in the Lord has sustained us through times of trial, sorrow, and upheaval.

My mother, Evelyn, was the youngest of Hattie Parker's seven children. My grandmother died in 1956. My mother was heartbroken after her mother passed away. She talked of her often when we were together, sharing stories of Hattie and what an amazing woman she had been as well as how much she loved her. Unfortunately, since I wasn't born until 1963, I never had the chance to know my grandmother.

1963 Little Known Fact: In 1963, Dr. King and the SCLC decided to turn their attention to Birmingham, Alabama's largest city and one of the industrial centers of the South. Local civil rights leader Fred Shuttlesworth, minister of the city's First Baptist Church, labeled it "the most segregated city in the United States."

Source: *Atlas of African-American History ... revised edition by James Ciment*

The stories of my Grandmother Hattie, which I can now remember, convince me that feisty, independent little Sharon Lee may have had much in common with her. I also know as a full-grown woman, I have many wonderful genetic traits from both my mother and grandmother. I am so happy to be able to remember my rich heritage and have the confidence to share it.

"If you have no confidence in self you are twice defeated in the race of life. With confidence, you have won even before you have started."

—Marcus Garvey

My mother told me that she was a *good girl* while growing up under Hattie Parker's roof and did everything her mother told her to do, wanting to follow in her footsteps and reflect her image.

Evelyn Parker, however, was emotionally devastated by having to leave her home and the events that followed concerning the Parker property. It has taken me many decades to realize that I wasn't the only one in the family severely traumatized by the fire. Maybe this was why I didn't see my mother for months, which had felt like years to me, after we had to leave our beloved home.

My mother had nine children living with her on the Parker Estate: Clifton, Kathy, Leo, Tracy, Patty, Darlene, Bridgette, and myself, *little Sharon Lee.* Lynn had not yet been born, and my oldest sister, Delores Parker Hawkins, had married and moved away. We would lose my younger brother Tony while in transition.

**Some of my siblings (Leo, Clifton, Tracy, Darlene, and Lynn—
others will be shared later in this Book.**

I was an extremely shy and quiet child, partly because of my introverted personality and partly because of the trauma that affected all of us, but I now know it affected my mother the most. Even though I was deeply hurt and confused by many unanswered questions, I was too scared and shy to ask them out loud. I didn't understand the weight of responsibility that was on my mother's shoulders. I also wasn't aware that there were other family matters angering, depressing, and upsetting my mother. I'm not sure whether she blamed herself or others … or perhaps, both?

I stood in the background and observed everything going on around me. As time went on, my list of questions grew and someday I would get all the answers, but it would be a long time before everything would become clear:

1. What or who caused the fire?

2. Why did so many strange, auspicious occurrences keep happening to me?

3. Why was I, Sharon Lee, chosen to represent the family and reclaim Hattie Parker's legacy?

4. Why did God keep spearing my life with directions I didn't want to follow?

5. Why, when I grew up, did I pursue the quest to learn all I could about African-American history, culture, and heritage?

While my mother was going through the initial shock and tough decisions in the aftermath of the fire, I was too young to understand why we had to move so often. I went through the motions, however, following my mother and siblings and doing what I was told. At least for six or seven years until I couldn't stand it anymore and started running away. It wouldn't be until much later in life that I would turn again to God for the answers.

I do have to share with everyone that my mother has been *"my rock"* for my entire life. *She let me be me!* She probably knew she'd never be able to change me.

My mother taught me to stay focused and encouraged me to develop my intelligence, wanting me to become the *"smart little girl"* that she believed Sharon Lee could be. Ms. Evelyn knew that her adventurous, rebellious, hard-headed, and very independent little girl would run into many pitfalls before achieving the path in life that would lead Sharon Lee back to Prince Frederick and the family home.

My mother released me to the world at the tender age of twelve to find my own way. I believe she knew exactly what she was doing, and it was done in love and with respect.

I thank my mother for this. I was a lot like her, I guess, for her to realize that I had to learn things the hard way so that it would *stick!* I experienced the trials and tribulations that she knew I would, but I would equip myself with the skills and *tough skin* I would need to overcome all the struggles, obstacles, and roadblocks on the pathway to my destiny, including The Original Parker Family Destiny.

My dear mother, Ms. Evelyn Parker, passed away in 2010.

"Thank you, Mom, I love you..."

—Sharon Parker

Chapter Six

The Harrowing Auspicious Occurrence

"Children see things very well sometimes—
and idealists even better!"

—Lorraine Hansberry

The year was 1973 and I was ten years old (another multiple of 5) when I found out something unsettling and shocking from my past … *you guessed it! From 1968 when I was five years old … a harrowing auspicious occurrence.*

Over the years, the older kids in the family would notice how much my mother had changed from the tender, loving parent she had been while living on the Parker Estate to a woman filled with anger and depression. They knew that our mother still loved us, but the sequence of bad luck and unfair, dirty dealings behind the scenes was taking a toll on my mother's emotions and gentle disposition, but no one talked about any of this. At least, not with me.

I had been too young to remember much of the before-and-after effects on my mother, but mainly I was hiding behind the shadows and darkness that altered or blocked my memories. I knew my mother was a strong woman and I never questioned her love for me, even though there were times when my shy, fearful nature made me wary of everyone, especially my family. We were packed into way too close quarters and just barely surviving from the tragedies that had only brought us heartbreak and loss.

Even though some headway had been made in the equal treatment of others, all minority groups including women, it really hadn't reached our little backwoods town as African-Americans were leaving Prince Frederick and Calvert County in huge numbers looking for a better way of life. It certainly hadn't helped any of the Parker family in 1973.

1970-1979 Little Known Facts: 1. Thomas Bradley is elected mayor of Los Angeles. Bradley is the first African-American to hold this position and is reelected four times, holding his position for 20 years. 2. The National Black Feminist Organization is developed by Eleanor Holmes Norton. 3. The Children's Defense Fund is established by Marion Wright Edelman. 4. Maynard H. Jackson, Jr. is elected as the first African-American mayor of Atlanta. 5. Coleman Young becomes the first African-American mayor of Detroit.

Source: http://afroamhistory.about.com/od/timelines/fl/African-American-History-Timeline-1970-to-1979.htm

On this auspicious day, *"Amee" (how we all referred to my Mom as kids)* called us girls—Patty, Darlene, Bridgette, Lynn, and Sharon Lee—to walk down to Aunt Elizabeth's house with her. I remembered dreading the walk down Adelina Road because we would have to pass by the land where the Parker Estate had once been. This was all so confusing to me for I knew my older brothers and sisters remembered something very different about the field with the trailer on it than I did. I just didn't know what it was.

All of us girls knew, however, *Amee* would start complaining and get extremely upset when we passed in front of this piece of land. I was completely in the dark and of course, I wanted to ask her, *"What was wrong?"* At 10 years old, I knew that would only upset her more. We just didn't talk about these things.

Anyone who knew my mother was aware that she was *old school,* probably like my Grandmother Hattie must have been. She wouldn't take lightly to her children asking her questions which were *"none of our concern."* My mother never really said anything. She wouldn't allow herself to express exactly what she was thinking and feeling—that's how a *lady* conducted herself—but the looks on her face told it all. *She didn't like something or someone who was living on the property.*

When we finally made it to my Aunt Elizabeth's residence, there was a close family friend there visiting with our Aunt. Her name was Valerie Hampton. As soon as I quietly crept into the room, she pointed at me and said, ***"That's my baby girl ... I saved you from the fire! She was the only one left in the house, and I ran back in the house to get her!"***

When I heard those words for the first time, I was confused and baffled: *"What fire? When? Where? And why was I left in the house?"* I had totally blacked out everything, but please remember, I never knew the reason why I had to go to that awful, run-down house all by myself.

No one in my family had ever told me about the fire in the kitchen of the Parker Estate—not my mother, my father, my brothers or sisters. Maybe they thought I was just too young and wouldn't have understood what was going on. But finding out about the fire at the age of ten really disturbed me. I know upon hearing her words that I didn't even respond to Ms. Valerie. I was completely traumatized *again.*

Valerie Hamilton and Johnny Brooks, 2017

I listened as my guardian angel told us that her hands had been burned in the fire when she ran back in the house to rescue me. I didn't even realize at the time that the scars on my stomach and under my right breast were from what must have been horrible burns. The scars that are still on my body to this day. Now, it makes sense, but nothing made sense to me on that day, so long ago. I was suffering from Shock Trauma from hearing this news and didn't even know it! No one did because my labored breaths wouldn't allow me to speak, but everyone was used to my shyness.

During this revelation, I think I was grateful to Ms. Valerie, my guardian angel, for saving my life, but I don't remember whether I was able to say anything to her that day or not. I'm very thankful now and know that God was looking out for me, but from this moment on, my life changed forever.

The Shock caused me to feel dizzy, befuddled, scared. I remember trying to keep my hands and body from shaking; my lips trembled; the tears that etched a pathway down my face were not happy tears as Valerie and my Aunt Elizabeth suspected, but rather tears of betrayal and revulsion.

Aunt Mary Elizabeth Willett

I immediately felt unloved and unwanted—*"Had everyone wanted me to die?"* Thinking in the mind of a 10-year-old but really, I flung myself emotionally back to the time of the fire, and I was five years old again in my damaged psyche.

Slowly yet consistently, I began to disconnect and disassociate myself from everyone in my family. I asked myself over and over again: *"Why me? Why was I left in the house? Where was my mother?—"Amee, help me!"* I wanted *to scream. Why didn't my brothers and sisters come to my aid? What would have happened to me if Ms. Valerie hadn't gone back in the house to save me?"*

No matter how hard I tried to forget—because *forgetting everything* was all I wanted to do—the questions would continue to surface in my head for years, but not too many years. Finally, I succeeded in totally blacking out everything that I couldn't remember. I was numb for four decades.

"There comes a time when silence is betrayal."

—Dr. Martin Luther King, Jr.

Chapter Seven

From Tomboy to Rebel-Rouser

"Children can't help the family they're born into and they sure can't pick their parents."

—Wise Old Saying

After I decided to leave my family behind, I turned into a very different child than the quiet, shy, little girl I had been at our small, cluttered shack. Maybe I was making up for lost time or maybe I was going to show the world that I was tough, strong, and stubborn. I wasn't going to let anyone hurt me or keep me in the dark again!

I was a true tomboy at heart, rightfully earning the nickname *Sharon Lee.* I remember riding my bike with no hands, fighting boys in school and winning, and running away from home for years.

Although my mother knew I was a smart little girl, I didn't know it. I played my way through school from kindergarten to the 12th grade. I believe my teachers only passed me through each year to get me out of their classroom and out of their hair. So, I went from grade-to-grade without learning anything. At least that's what I thought.

I share this because I didn't think I was worth anything to anyone. That's the reason I've been so uncomfortable about writing this book on my life, but I strongly feel that there are other little girls out there who are five years old or remember how lost and alone they felt at five years old that need the courage and confidence to become someone who can change the world!

I realize that it wasn't all my fault. I know my family meant well, but they too must take some responsibility for what I went through at an early age, which grew into a big chip on my shoulder and a total lack of trust in not just my family, but everyone.

"If only we could have talked it all out.
Yeah, if only, if only… Thank goodness,
I had God and His Angels watching over me
or I would never have made it through everything,
but I could never admit it during my rebellious years.
I would never let anyone see me hurt or see me cry."

—Sharon Parker

I was forced to raise myself from the age of twelve, which no child is equipped to do, even though we may think we are. But I really didn't have a choice. That's right, my mother, father, nor my older siblings were around enough to teach me right from wrong, the importance and sanctity of life, or keep me from going down the wrong path.

In fairness, I must say that my oldest sister Patty tried to fill the void of mother for me, but she was just too demanding. I couldn't wait until she had her own family to bully. At least that's how I felt about it then. There's only so much a shy and quiet person can take before the noise and commotion causes her to break into a rip-roaring fight!

Parker Family Story: *We were all getting ready for school one morning, and Patty and I were still upset from a fight the night before. She had told me it was my turn to do the dishes. I said it wasn't. Patty charged me and started hitting me. I responded in kind and kicked her ---- you know what. The next morning, we were at it again because even though she was older, the tough tomboy Sharon Lee kicked her butt all the time. This particular morning, we were kicking, hitting, and clawing with no clothes on, and my other siblings were cracking up. They just couldn't quit laughing at us two angry, uninhibited fools!*

We all knew that *Aimee* was just too emotionally overwhelmed to take care of all of us. She never recovered from the anger of losing her beloved mother's home. She took to drinking when she went out walking up and down Adelina Road, past the property and the trailer. She just couldn't stay away from that field; sometimes walking or stumbling down that narrow road even late at night.

I would often hear my mother complaining over and over again about some lady living on the Parker's Estate. She would say in a raised voice, ***"… she knock down my mother's home!"*** She would get so upset, and I could see the pain on her face when she'd been drinking … repeating the same thing again and again. Too young to understand or even care, I didn't know what to do. So, I ran away.

Those unforgiveable escapades of moving from house-to-house, family-to-family, played an intricate part in my disconnect with my family. I'd tell any story I had to tell to get my friends and their families to take me in. *I just didn't care, and I didn't want to be a part of the Parker family.*

During my whole life growing up on Adelina Road, I heard the old tales of a Parker family member stealing my

Grandmother Hattie Parker's land and that my own father helped this woman. I heard these rumors even when I was living with someone else. I was so disgusted with all this neighborhood gossip about my family and watched as my mother tried to drink her pain away; everyone talking about my mother as well, shaking their heads and saying how sad it was, even as they condemned her actions. I just couldn't take it anymore!

I decided I didn't want anything to do with the Parker family, the land or their legacy. I knew absolutely nothing about my Ancestors, the Estate, the house or the rich history that dated back to when most African-Americans were slaves. I didn't even know my great-grandparents' names, nor did I want to know anything about them or any other member of the family. *I didn't want to be a Parker in Prince Frederick, Maryland!*

My plans were to leave my home in Calvert County for **good** as soon as I was old enough; that's exactly what I did, but there were more hurdles to jump before I could escape.

"Your silence will not protect you."

—Audre Lorde

Chapter Eight

Being on the Wrong Path

"You really need to be careful of who you hang out with and who you listen to. They can lead you down the wrong path."

—Demi Lovato

From the moment that I became a teenager at 13 years old, I took that first step on *"the wrong path."* I ran away from home to stay with my best friend in Lusby, Maryland, not far from Prince Frederick, but a world away from my home life.

Sandra Buck and I were two wild girls who had a great time getting into trouble. I spent two summers in Lusby with Sandra, only going home occasionally to hide when the trouble we were in was too much for me to handle.

When I was just barely 15 years old, I met a boy at a party in Sandra's house where I was living. I'd been seeing him around the neighborhood in Lusby, and we got involved *'hot and heavy'* from that night on. I had the biggest crush on him. He was a few years older than I was and made me feel very grown up. I think he may have been 17 years old.

Not long afterwards was one of those times when I went back home. I wasn't feeling well and wasn't getting any better like I'd always done before when I had partied too much or had a cold, "bug", or the flu. My mother took me to our family doctor, whose office was also in Lusby. When the doctor solemnly said, *"She is with child,"* you should have seen the look on my mother's face? It was an expression of total shock and disappointment. After my mother composed herself, she said to the doctor, *"What did you say?"* There was total silence between us from the time we left the doctor's office until we got home.

Sharon and 5-year Tonique

Looking back, I don't understand why my mother was so shocked since I'd been allowed to be away from home for as long as I could remember. I'd had no supervision and was only vaguely aware of the consequences of my actions. I really wasn't much more than a *child* myself.

This turned out to be a turning point in my life—an auspicious occurrence to make me grow up? I was going to bring a new life into this world. I was only in the 11th grade, but I had to face my responsibilities. I moved back home.

I realized early on that my daughter, Tonique D. Parker, has a strong destiny to fulfill. She has been my light and blessing from the moment I first held her in my arms. *Perhaps this was God's way of cherishing this earth with Tonique's beautiful soul* **and would get my life back on track.**

Perhaps … perhaps not … for I would make other questionable choices before I found the pathway that God had predestined for me when I was only five years old. I had yet to receive the answer to my burning question.

I met my high school sweetheart after Tonique was born. I left home again to stay with him and his family in District Heights, near Forestville, Maryland. It was a wonderful experience for me, living in what seemed to me a *"big city."*

My mother didn't know how to drive a car so we'd never gone on family vacations, out-of-town or to see relatives. The only time I ever left Calvert County was on field trips.

As soon as I graduated from Calvert High in 1982, I left and never looked back, only occasionally coming home on a holiday to visit my mother and family. Prince Frederick's lifestyle was too slow for me, too much a rural farming community. Most importantly, there were no job opportunities and career advancement for African-Americans in my hometown. I did everything in my power not to be associated with anything that reminded me of my childhood, which had caused me so much pain.

It was a conscious decision on my part to completely disconnect myself from the place I had never felt a connection with. I believed that I didn't truly belong on Adelina Road Prince Frederick, Calvert County, Maryland.

"You can't leave your behavior and habits behind."

—Sharon Parker

Maybe I was a fool to think that my life was going to miraculously change by leaving my hometown where everyone knew the Parker name and history. I could hide from my memories and the past, but I continued to make some of the same mistakes in my choice of boyfriends. I was a young woman and wanted to have a good time. It had become a way of life. The only difference was that I didn't have to run away anymore, but I didn't have any place to go back to when I got into trouble either. I was on my own.

Don't get me wrong, I had lots of fun and excitement, but I was the girl who'd always had the freedom to do anything I wanted and go anywhere since I was twelve years old. My behavior and habits would continue to drag me down for way over a decade.

I was the same stubborn, active, and free-spirited person I'd always been, but being an introvert, there are some advantages to being shy and quiet. I reverted back to the child standing in the shadows, listening and observing everything and everyone around me. I knew how to quickly piece things together and solve problems. This helped me to understand myself and my mother. Since I was a mother now too, I was able to *"get"* what she'd been going through. As an adult, I no longer blamed *Amee* for **my** mistakes.

I lived a hard-knock life after I graduated from high school and was on my own near the big city of Washington, D.C. It was 1999, and I had four beautiful, wonderful daughters. We were a family when I bought us a home in Clinton, Maryland, but things were tough; the five of us were alone; and I was stuck in *survival-mode.* I knew how my mother must have felt when all twelve of us had been dependent upon her when our whole lives fell apart. I didn't want to repeat this same pattern.

I finally came to my senses and knew I had to focus on my personal life and professional career. I asked myself, *"What kind of legacy was I going to leave for my children and their children if I didn't clean up my act?"*

You get out of life what you put into it, and even though I never lost my faith in God, I wasn't letting Him call the shots either. I guess I didn't know how to let go and let Him guide me through uncharted waters. It would take more auspicious occurrences for me to find my way.

But I believe that everything happens for a reason. I want to thank the people who tried to control me; those who did me wrong; those who took me for granted; and those who didn't believe in me. These people fueled the fires that burned in me to overcome my struggles and challenges. I wanted to prove them all wrong—Sharon Lee was just as strong ever!

There were some good people put in my pathway through the grace of God who helped me along the way, but they were few and far between. I know my hardships were caused by my own stubbornness, and I didn't have anyone in my life to direct me down the right path.

"If you're walking down the right path and you're willing to keep walking eventually you'll make progress."

—President Barack Obama, 44th U.S. President

Sharon Finds Self Through ROASA, Inc.

Chapter Nine

Auspicious Occurrences

"Don't look back. Something may be gaining on you!"

—Satchel Paige

When I made the decision to point my life and career in a more positive direction for myself and my daughters, I had no idea that I would need to make a U-turn and return to my roots, my home, to find the pathway from the past that would unlock my memories, answer my question from 1968, reveal my true purpose, and set me on a new course for the future.

For my whole life, I have always had what I refer to as *"auspicious occurrences"* with intuitive, inner knowing that I believe are messages from God.

I remember having vivid dreams that I shared with my brothers and sisters when we were just children. My children always did what I told them to do to prevent mishap. We all believed in my dreams because *they came true.*

Most of these night-time messages were about someone who was in danger or about to get seriously injured or killed in an accident. I couldn't have lived with myself if I didn't intervene and find a way to warn them to make sure they would be in a different place, at a different time. I would first pray to God to spare their lives, asking Him to protect them, and then call the person directly to encourage them to change their plans and schedule for the next day.

I strongly believe those dreams were a test from God to see if I was listening to the inner-gifts and blessings He was bestowing upon me. The Lord was preparing me for the journey that would lead me to the discovery of His destiny for me. From an early age, these dreams let me know that I would always be involved with helping other people.

After my daughter Tonique had grown up and left home, I would call her to meet me for breakfast, lunch, but mostly dinner to talk about something unusual that had happened to me or a series of strange occurrences from the previous day or week.

We would order a drink to relax and then our meal, but the real conversation always began with me saying, *"You are not going to believe this ..."* Many times, I would start off by relating a dream to her.

Tonique, as I wrote about in *The Introduction* to this book, has been the person in my life who helped me the most to decipher the blocked-out memories and *auspicious occurrences* that led me to:

"Pathway to My True Purpose: *Recovery-to-Discovery"*

—Sharon Parker, author

"True Synergy Works ... Leading Within!"

As God prepared me for this miraculous change in direction to come, he dropped another *"jewel"* into my lap to see if I was paying attention. My dear, dear friend, Shebah Aqeel, was as close to me as any sister, and this is how I referred to her before she passed, leaving this world to dwell with God's Angels. *"May she rest in peace..."*

In 2003, I purchased a picture for Shebah that showed two beautiful African-American children, one girl and one boy ready for bed in front of an open book with images in a circle behind their heads revealing the history of Africans coming to America under threat of death (an old flintlock pistol) with the wheel of a slave ship and possibly the children's Ancestors, many generations removed, as well as great people of color in Civil Rights and other historical significance. I had no idea why I bought this sacred example of family and history, but God knew that it was the next step

I needed to take to reach back to my heritage. Sharing it with my *dear sister Shehah Aqeel* only made it more precious.

Shebah was my mentor, and in her gracious humility, she didn't even know it. For once in my life, up to this point, my hardheaded self just listened ... and learned.

I gained so much insight from her loving wisdom on life, current and evolving social consciousness, trends in media and commercialism that kept people divided, reacting only from greed and selfishness for money, pleasure, instant gratification, lack of self-control; even how families became disconnected—angry, vengeful, and hateful to the very ones we should be able to turn to when we need love and support as we are to be there for them. She showed me how to treasure and share my faith with others.

She taught me so much more. I could just go on and on. Just by talking to me about herself and seemingly random acts of kindness and inspiration, I know God placed her in my path at just the right time, giving of herself, just what I needed. I miss *my wise sister* terribly, but I know she looks down upon me from heaven. I want to make her proud of me.

It wasn't until 2007 that God would allow me to remember the unexplainable incidents that had spanned over 40 years of my life. I was a grandmother when I finally accepted the course God had predestined for me when I was five-year-old *Sharon Lee,* playing in the churchyard field across the street from a plot of land with a trailer on it, when I asked an important question to God.

Even then, in 1968, I felt I was supposed to bring people together in love and harmony, lending a helping hand to people in need. Over 30 years later, this would lead me to become an employee for the United States Federal Government, the Department of Housing and Urban Development (HUD).

Along the way, however, instead of connecting with people, I disconnected from my family, my community, but especially with *myself.*

I wholeheartedly believe that God gave me the courage and faith to recall these repressed memories and unlock the secrets of my *auspicious occurrences,* connecting the pieces so I could remember the facts I needed to reclaim my family's legacy, but there are more surprises yet to come!

I didn't know that I had an inspirational *"voice"* that had been dormant and unused for such a long time. I never made a conscious decision to find and release this voice, but it had never been up to me. It was given to me by God. Stubborn, hard-headed Sharon Parker, *kicking and screaming every step of the way,* finally saw that I was being called, but I had to answer that call and do my share. It was the hardest work I'd ever done to research and understand the African-American heritage, history, and contributions to our great country, the United States of America. It made me proud.

My own hometown of Prince Frederick would be even more complicated to unravel since the African-American roots of Calvert County is a unique, diversified hot-bed of history, dating back to the 17th century. This includes the legacy of *The Original Parker Family.*

In 2007, before my mother's passing, my siblings and I were told that we had lost our Grandmother Hattie Parker's land from the decision of a lawsuit against my mother, Evelyn Parker, and my Aunt Elizabeth. This lawsuit had been filed by another Parker family member.

Aunt Mary Elizabeth Parker-Willett and Sister, Evelyn M. Parker

2007 Little Known Fact: *In February 2007, just months after he became only the third African-American elected to the U.S. Senate since Reconstruction, Obama announced his candidacy for the 2008 Democratic presidential nomination.*

Source: http://www.history.com/topics/black-history/black-history-milestones

Part of my calling came "alive"—www.roasalives.org—in 2008, when I founded the not-for-profit organization, "Remembering Our Ancestors Synergistic Association, Inc." (ROASA).

"The impulse to dream had been slowly beaten out of me by experience. Now it surged up again and I hungered for books, new ways, of looking and seeing."

—Richard Wright

Chapter Ten

"Recovery-to-Discovery"
My Journey Back to the Past

"The life of the dead is placed
in the memory of the living."

—Marcus Tullius Cicero

My mother, dear *Amee,* passed away in 2010 due to kidney and liver failure. Again, I retreated into the darkness and shadows of my mind, but I couldn't allow myself to wallow in sadness and grief for long. I had important work to do.

My mom, Evelyn M. Parker with Friends

I had promised my mother that I would bring our family back together. *"Why me?"* I had wondered at the time because I had turned my back on the family and gone my own way. Powers from beyond the grave and from God in heaven were at work behind the scenes.

Little did I know the mountain of obstacles that would be placed in my pathway and that these challenges would make it almost impossible to keep that promise! But I kept putting one foot in front of the other, making the final burial arrangements for my mother because it had auspiciously fallen to me. Maybe it helped me to push myself up from the darkness and see the glow of my mother's afterlife that I so firmly believe in. The message and necessity of ROASA was never clearer in my mind than in this time of mourning, mixed with tears and the breakthrough of more memories.

While I was busy arranging, organizing, and graciously, yet gladly, doing my duty for my mother, who had been so tortured by family concerns for most of her life, all the issues that had divided the family rose to the surface. I remembered many *not-so-nice* people that fueled my spirit to fight beyond my shyness and quiet nature to harden and protect my heart by any means necessary from the pain, mental cruelty, and unfairness that had dominated my early years.

Reflecting back on this, even though it was an exhausting and emotionally draining time in my life, I can't thank God enough for my *not-so-easy* childhood. Those rough, hard-knock lessons only made me stronger and more stubborn about my beliefs. I became indebted to the people who came to me for advice and what *they* call my *"inner wisdom."*

I can't help but giggle with a big dose of humility when I hear these wonderful things said about the Sharon Parker of today. But, in 2010, this person was just beginning to evolve.

2010 Little Known Facts: In November 2010, Democrat Kamaia Harris wins election as California attorney general. In doing so, she becomes the first woman; first African-American and first Indian American in California history to be elected state attorney general.

February 27, 2010: A new visitor center opens in New York City, near the re-discovered 17th and 18th century burial ground of African, free and enslaved who helped create the nation's cultural and commercial capital."

Source: http://www.theroot.com/photos/black-history-month-time-line-50-years-of-black-histoyr/#slide-21

"The blood, sweat, tears, and suffering of Black people
are the foundation of the wealth and power of
The United States of America."

—Huey P. Newton

"Another auspicious occurrence? A few days before we
buried our mother, Patty handed me some property court
papers of a case filed in 1985 concerning my mother and
Aunt Elizabeth. Not sure what they meant, I put them in a
safe place; unconsciously, I knew they were important!"

—Sharon Parker

After my mother's funeral, I started working with other family members to plan our 2010 (another multiple of the number 5!) family reunion. I became one of the key committee members that would host our first Original Parker Family Reunion at a *'meet-and-greet'* in Calvert Country.

Here was the girl who never got involved in family matters and continually ran away from home since the age of twelve, but I took the extra step to create a Facebook group page for the family. My reason for getting involved besides the promise I'd made to my mother? I knew it was essential to expose my family and friends to ROASA, Inc., which is the African-American historical organization I had just created two years previously. *This is what "Ancestral Synergy" is all about!* The more I learned, the more I yearned for peace.

As I was planning, God was planning my pathway to destiny. During reunion preparations, I was asked to provide a family tree which would link Benjamin and Grace Parker, Jr. my great-grandparents, to the Parker descendants of Prince Frederick, Calvert County, Maryland. *Where had my great-grandparents come from?* More time would pass before I received the answer to this auspicious question.

This was the first indication I had that I was now on the path that I'd fought so hard and so long to ignore and obliterate from my life and mind. This was my initial step in getting to know myself. I walked forward, but in the midst of the excitement of discovery, I must admit there were times that I was afraid of the recovery.

"Challenges make you discover things about yourself that you never really knew."

—Cicely Tyson

Chapter Eleven

The Parker Family Land and Legacy

"The land is sacred; it belongs to the numbers
who are dead, the few who are living,
and the multitudes of those yet to be born."

—Penan

In June of 2012, another *auspicious occurrence* would set into motion revelations about my family and the field with the trailer from my 1968 memory. I came across a lady's name, Kirsdi Uunilla, in a flyer given to me by one of my cousins, Dawn Tucker, a business owner in Calvert County. This flyer announced an upcoming course on African-American history for residents of Calvert and Charles Counties. Since I was doing the same type of education in Prince George County, where I live, I wanted to collaborate with her.

I misplaced the flyer and couldn't remember the lady's name or phone number. Totally devastated, I reached out to Dawn, but she had accidently deleted the flyer from her hard drive.

I was so upset! This time I knew there was something important I needed to learn from Ms. Uunilla, but I was completely stymied.

A few months later, when I was in my hometown on business, it hit me that the lady teaching the course must work for the Calvert County Board of Education in the school system. I was surprised that this was being taught in 2012 because African-American history had never been addressed when I was in high school from 1979-1982. I also knew from my own research that the African-American population had decreased to only about 11%, but we had been in the majority back when African-Americans owned and worked their own land, prior to the 1970s.

By being diligent and calling the Board of Education, even though I couldn't even begin to remember or pronounce the lady's name, they transferred me to the middle school where I spoke to a man who taught Social Studies. Surprisingly, he knew her! He even had her phone number! God was looking out for me once again by putting the right people in my path at the right time. Her name, of course, was Kirsdi Uunilla, but she wasn't a teacher, but rather an archeologist for the Calvert County Planning and Zoning Office.

It took a few days to connect with Kirsdi. She was out of the office when I called, on vacation. I found out that she was uncovering the history of slaves in Calvert County. We set up a meeting for a few weeks later. The class I had seen advertised in the flyer was not being taught by Ms. Uunilla, but rather a professor from Charles County, Maryland, based on her research. It didn't matter whether we could collaborate on the African-American classes or not, I was very excited about meeting Ms. Uunilla.

What I didn't realize, however, was the incredible *auspicious occurrence* God had in store for me and the blessings I would receive. For on this *auspicious* day, God and Kirsdi Uunilla would give me the gift of my family's history!

We shared a cup of coffee, with it being warmed up a couple of times, as we spent much more time together than I would have imagined. It wasn't the number of minutes or hour of the clock; it was the meeting of a kindred spirit that gave of herself and her talents to a hesitant, confused woman on a personal, yet time-consuming, quest.

Kirsdi was metaphorically digging through online records to research the first slaves who had come to Calvert County and settled in Prince Frederick, particularly the landowners and farmers of Adelina Road, which was the cornerstone of the community. *Guess what name she shared with me as soon as she heard my last name? Yes, none other than "Parker!"*

I mentioned to her that I had brought with me some court papers from my deceased mother and my Aunt Elizabeth, who was still a resident of Prince Frederick. I told her I had an estate number from a property case that was filed back in 1985. *Would this help her to locate an old house that had been torn down? Yes, those same papers that Patty gave to me in 2010...the year my mother passed.*

Trying desperately to control my emotions, I was shocked after hardening my heart for so many decades that I still had tears to shed. I quieted myself and waited for her to check and see if there was any information to correspond with the estate number.

She went to her computer and pulled up an amazing satellite software package that showed houses and buildings that were once in Calvert County. As soon as she put in the estate number, a picture associated with the Parker Estate came up as my Ancestors' home.

The Day I Found My Ancestors' Home

I explained to Kirsdi that even though I had been very young at the time the house was destroyed, it was eerily familiar to me and I was almost 100 percent sure that it was the house my mother, Evelyn Parker, was living in at the time of my birth in 1963. I wanted to confirm it with my Aunt Elizabeth who was in the hospital near Kirsdi's office. She printed it off, and I headed for the hospital, which I had been planning on doing anyway while I was in Prince Frederick.

When I arrived at the hospital, it was an emotional reunion with Aunt Elizabeth who absolutely confirmed this was the Parker Estate belonging to Benjamin Parker. I couldn't wait to call Kirsdi and give her the news that it was indeed the home of The Original Parker Family of Adelina Road. I put my aunt Mary on the phone with Kirsdi Uunilla.

They talked for about 15 life-changing minutes. I couldn't believe how excited Aunt Elizabeth was as she shared stories about the house with Kirsdi, even down to the apple tree that had been planted in the front yard by my great-grandparents.

It was a wonderful day! I couldn't wait to tell my siblings, nieces, nephews, and cousins about how God had put Kirsdi Uunilla in my pathway to help me find our Ancestors' home.

I was so happy to see the picture of the beautiful house that *lit up the night* (Chapter Two) with compound lights on an electrical generator that was unheard on Adelina Road at the time, but I was the most surprised that I was positive I had seen that house before … in the back of mind, breaking through the clouds of my memories. The Lord was sending me the blessing of clarity.

> *"I said to De Lord, 'I'm Goin' To Hold Steady On To You, An' I Know You'll See Me Through!'"*

—Harriet Tubman

Chapter Twelve

Coming Full Circle
Sharon Lee Finds Her Home Again

"I want to be remembered as someone who used herself and anything she could touch to work for justice and freedom... I want to be remembered as one who tried."

—Dorothy Height

I wouldn't find out that there was unfinished work on the Parker legacy until 2013, three years after my mother's death. Even though I had become more involved in the lives of my family members, the promise I had made to my mother of reuniting the family was but a shadow and promise of what was to come.

It started with a written secret and advanced into one of the most difficult periods of my life. *Sharon Lee* may have believed as a child that she didn't know right from wrong, but somewhere along the way her belief in truth and justice had become one of the most important synergistic principles

I would pass onto patrons and recipients of my non-profit organization, ROASA, Inc.

One Christmas eve of 2013 my siblings and I received a certified letter from a Calvert County lawyer representing a family member to notify us that we would have to reclaim some of the family property that was part of the Benjamin and Grace Parker, Sr. Estate, *legal* original owners per Calvert County records. The deed is erroneously in Benjamin, Sr.'s name referring to Benjamin, Jr. born in 1865, rather than Benjamin, Sr. born 1828, due probably to the fire in the courthouse where deeds and other important papers were destroyed. I have to be honest and confess that I had no desire to reclaim *any* portion of the Parker land. I had grown up with all this buzzing in my ears of convoluted gossip and over-dramatized stories. I'd heard way too much about it, but God had other plans for me and my family.

I realize now why I was being directed back to the past to reclaim not just the land, but my rightful place in the Parker family. At the end of the Parker Reunion in 2010, I reconnected with family who I'd had no interaction with for quite a long time.

After the reunion, I was on Adelina Road visiting my aunt and first cousin Mary Willet, rekindling old ties, and they brought up the fact that *all* of our land had been taken by another Parker family member. At the time, I didn't even know what the property consisted of—I only knew about the trailer on the plot of land across the road from the church, the field that had always upset and depressed my mother so much. I blamed that piece of land for my mother's drinking that ultimately led to her death.

I politely listened to the stories that I'd heard so many times before, but I didn't pay too much attention. I was tired of hearing about this land, and I didn't want anything to do with all the controversy. My life had taken a very different path, and I thought I was doing what I was meant to do. Little did I know that God was going to bring me full circle back to the beginning where five-year old Sharon Lee was playing across the street and had asked God, *"Why?"*

If the rumors were true, then the one-acre where the Parker house had once stood *may* still have been available to descendants of Hattie Parker, my grandmother, along with an additional five acres (my special number of 5).

A few weeks later, I received a strange phone call from Aunt Elizabeth telling me that the Parker Estate was listed in the newspaper in a tax sale. That call changed my ability to make a choice in this matter. These back-taxes were attached to my grandmother's estate and therefore to her children, which included me. I contacted my older brother Leo to have him confirm this information.

Well, as you can probably imagine, it was true. Leo, my younger sister Lynn, and I paid the taxes for 2008, 2009, and 2010. It was believed that the family member once living in the trailer intentionally stopped paying the taxes so the estate would go into a "tax sale" where she and her family could purchase it when the bank foreclosed on the property.

I brought out those tax and legal papers that my oldest sister Patty had given me right before my mother's funeral. Yes, those papers gave us a second chance to reclaim the land upon which the Parker Estate had been located as descendants of Hattie Parker.

Lynn arranged a meeting with an attorney for the three of us (Leo, Lynn, and myself). Even though I was willing to assist in this process, I never intended to spearhead the effort. This was to be a fact-finding mission, and I told them both that I did not want to lead the fight. I lived too far away; I was too busy; I had a career and a company to run as well as affiliations with numerous African-American groups, including at that time, Commissioner of Maryland African-American History and Culture.

Lynn and I had a disagreement on this subject the morning of the meeting and she didn't show. She gave Leo and me no warning. She called the attorney's office just a few minutes before the scheduled time for the meeting, telling the law office that she couldn't show up in-person, and asked to be included by phone on a conference-call. Needless to say, I was very upset.

Just a few minutes into the meeting, the attorney informed us that they had not been able to locate either of my mother and aunt's case files for 1985 or 2007.

"At that moment, I knew I would be returning to my hometown because I thought it was a conspiracy in the 'good-old-boys-club' and legal system of Calvert County."

—Sharon Parker

I, of course, had brought the property papers with me to the meeting and was able to show the attorney a copy of the 1985 case they had not been able to locate. The rest of the meeting was double-talk saying more research was needed; they had to go to the courthouse to see what was actually filed and get the jury's ruling on the case; they'd get back with us in a few days. Days turned into weeks and phone calls went unanswered or I was told they hadn't gotten the information.

My sister and I were still not speaking. It seemed that this tax situation was never going to be resolved. I got angry and called my Prepaid Legal attorney. I was told to contact the Register of Wills for Calvert County, which I did. The receptionist said I needed to speak with Margaret Phipps. It was two days before Christmas, and it took me all afternoon to get in touch with her.

When I heard her gentle country voice on the phone, it calmed me down considerably. I asked about becoming the personal representative (PR) to the Benjamin and Grace Parker, Sr. estate. She told me that she recalled the name, and I was excited to hear that. For a few minutes, I forgot about the property situation and focused on wanting to know more about my Ancestors. I learned the dates of when my great-grandfather, great-grandmother, and grandmother had died. In that moment, they became *real people* to me and I felt they were asking for my help from the afterlife.

I was at my office in Washington, D.C., when I asked Ms. Phipps if I could get copies of the Will since I was coming to Calvert County on that day. I left at shortly after 3:00 p.m. and arrived at the courthouse in Prince Frederick at 4:15. On the drive, my sister Lynn, who I hadn't spoken to in weeks, called to let me know the attorney was on the way to the courthouse to find out if my mother's case had been officially filed. An auspicious occurrence? Was God guiding me?

When I met with Ms. Phipps. I was surprised how much she knew about the Parker estate. I told her that I was one of the heirs and what I was attempting to do. She provided me with the Wills and told me more about my family than I'd ever heard from anyone else. She told me to engage an attorney as soon as possible. She knew about the case because just a few days earlier the other family member who resided on that plot of land had obtained an attorney and asked about the same part of the Parker property. This infuriated me. The quest to reclaim my mother's portion of the estate was now my crusade and little Sharon Lee was ready!

After the meeting, I remember Lynn telling me that the attorney who had represented my mother and aunt in 1985 had gone to the courthouse that very day and their office was just across the street from the courthouse. So, I'm sure you don't have to guess who marched across the street and into that law office.

After waiting to talk to the attorneys, a daughter and her father, the elder stated that the case had not been filed and he didn't remember any of the details. We would have to start from the very beginning in the process of creating a deed for the portion of land in Hattie Parker's Will, which was over six acres of the original 44 acres of land. This would bring the family back together in the fight of our lives, led by a stubborn, independent, quiet little girl who had asked at the tender, innocent age of 5 in 1968 near the *auspicious place*:

> *"God, why is it that blacks are hated by whites*
> *and why do we struggle so much?"*

> —*Little Sharon Lee*

Section II

Sharon Parker

"What Dwells Within..."

Chapter Thirteen

Sharon Parker ... All Grown Up!

"Learn to be quiet enough to hear the genuine within yourself so that you can hear it in others."

—Marian Wright Edelman

How did the memory of myself at five years old lead me to break through the blocks which would allow me to know myself, my true self—the soul God had bestowed on me before I drew my first breath, before I was even born? And if this predestined soul could lift me up out of the mire that had been my life, could I feel this resonance in others and guide them too?

This is what started to come together as I became a woman with plans, dreams, and ideals; the metamorphosis from Sharon Lee, the headstrong child, to Sharon Parker, an adult with defined goals and a passion for leadership.

As a shy little girl in 1968, I was standing in sight of my forefather's property and legacy on Adelina Road, Prince Frederick, Maryland. It was as if the land, which had been the home of my Ancestors for countless generations before my own, called to me and I responded in my heart and soul.

In a moment of *Grace* as a mere child, I became the land and the land became me as I voiced a poignant question fueled by my innocence and faith in God. My inner mind was crying out:

Why was life such a struggle? Why were people treated differently if we were all the same in God's eyes? Why didn't other races get along, especially white people who hated black people they didn't even know? And why did African-Americans have to suffer so much?

"The land and synergy of my Ancestors seeped into my being, becoming one with me. It would take over forty years for me to know what had taken root inside of me."

—Sharon Parker, reflecting on her first memory

I believe and have always believed, even in my rebellious teenage years, that God heard the question of a scared, unsettled five-year-old and placed me on a path from which I would run and hide, but with adulthood the truth inside me would become my life's quest.

To accept the knowledge and inner gifts given to me by God, however, my unconscious repressed and consciously suppressed memories would need to be reached for me to access the beauty of *"What Dwells Within."*

People say that you know your own destiny and that may be true unless you're like I was in 1968—a stubborn, independent child who had to learn everything the hard way with no parental guidance during my formative childhood and adolescent years.

With time and growth, shedding the persona of *Sharon Lee* and accepting the identity of *Sharon Parker*, the search for what was already a part of me was one of the hardest things I have ever done. But everything happens for a reason, and the reason was to prepare me for the journey that would alter my life and the lives of others.

"Every people should be originators of their own destiny."

—Martin Delaney

Chapter Fourteen

Perception, Persuasion, Remembrances

*"I wasn't concerned about the hardships because I
always felt I was doing what I had to do,
what I wanted to do and what I was destined to do."*

—Katherine Dunham

Since you've already read my past as five-year-old Sharon Lee, it's time to introduce you to Sharon Parker, President and founder of Remembering Our Ancestors Synergistic Association, Inc., (ROASA) a non-profit organization; former Commissioner of the Maryland Commission of African-American History and Culture; United States Federal Government Program Manager for the Department of Housing and Urban Development (HUD), celebrating my 30-year tenure in March 2017; President of the Maryland's Chapter of American Mothers, Inc.; and President of the Robert C. Weaver, Blacks in Government.

I'm the mother of four beautiful daughters and have seven amazing grandchildren. *The hardship and hard work has been much, but "Yes," I have indeed been blessed!*

"The African-American experience is one of the most important threads in the American tapestry."

—Bill Frist

As a federal government employee, I have heard and seen this famous quote many times by Dr. William Harrison "Bill" Frist, physician; heart and lung transplant surgeon; businessman; and later politician, Majority Leader of the Senate from 2003-2007.

I liked what it said and, believe you me, I noticed when I chose this quote to introduce the new direction I would undertake in the auspicious year of 2003 that my cycles of five were intact (2 + 3 = 5), just as my 30-year anniversary with HUD was a multiple of my special number. 2003 was the year I realized that I had to leave my own legacy for my daughters and grandchildren. I wasn't happy with where I'd been and, consequently, where I was headed.

I wasn't totally cognizant, either, that I had to become whole and complete within myself before I could even attempt to guide my loved ones, and the concept of "synergy" creating *much* more out of the scattered parts of my psyche was auspiciously 5 years in the future.

Little did I know I would have to go back to the past to take control of the present before I could even begin to grasp the synergistic movement growing in my subconscious mind which would become ROASA, Inc., I would have to accept what I was really made of to deal with my perceptions, persuasions, and remembrances … all of them!

I had never pieced together *the tapestry* to connect the *threads* of the past, nor given much thought to the complexity of the African-American *experience*. I was too busy putting one-foot-in-front-of-the-other to get me and my family through each day.

Who did I think I was, still clinging to poor little five-year-old Sharon Lee, to expect that I could make a difference in the lives of other people when I wasn't doing so well with my own?

www.roasalives.org would become my mission to help others avoid the pitfalls that I had fallen into, and I'm here to tell you that anyone, ***everyone***, has what it takes to change the world. We all have a purpose and a role to play.

I never dreamed when I initially perceived the synergy of ROASA in 2007, becoming entrepreneur of my own company a year later, that such creativity could spring forth from my analytical mind. 2007 became the year when I would sweep the cobwebs out of my head and begin to remember and listen to the auspicious messages and gifts from God.

Little Known Fact of 2007: *Barack Obama has won two Grammy Awards. He was first honored in 2005 for the audio version of his memoir, Dreams from My Father (best spoken word album), and received his second Grammy (in the same category) in 2007 for his political work, The Audacity of Hope.*

Source: Westside Gazette, Broward County [Fort Lauderdale, Florida] Oldest and Largest African-American Owned and Operated Newspaper, 46 Years, 1971-2017.

The key to hearing our Maker's words is in all of us. The hardest part, once you delve deep enough to connect with that soft lingering voice which grows in strength and volume as you nourish it, is that it does no good unless you ***accept*** the inner core beliefs of your being.

Acceptance is understanding, forgiveness, and for me, ***"… reaching out to take the hand of God,"*** by whatever name you call your higher power who blessed you with life and gave you the pathway to your true purpose and destiny.

It's all there, dwelling within you, waiting to be unleashed, but there are some major obstacles to overcome before you can access the spiritual wisdom that we are born with. We will also be given an abundance of gifts and an outpouring of inspirational creativity if we allow ourselves to seek and then listen to the voice within us.

Yet first, I had to listen to my own perceptions and the persuasions that altered those perceptions by justifying my own actions to myself and others before I could reach the remembrances locked away in the inner recesses of my mind.

Separating truth from myth was my biggest stumbling block. How can any of us trust the validity of what we remember? Every time a family story is retold, it's changed by the speaker's perceptions and persuasive arguments to put the narrator "in a good light," so to speak.

Memories are like dreams—misty and cloudy, totally distorted beyond recognition or simply gone, faded into darkness. All I could remember for decades was pain and wanting to escape Calvert County, Maryland.

It's important for me to share at this point, being the *"Memoir of The Original Parker Family,"* that a family member rewrote our family history through the power of perception, persuasion, and remembrances, convincing the whole town of a reality that never truly existed.

"Hate is too great a burden to bear. It injures the hater more than it injures the hated."

—Coretta Scott King

Chapter Fifteen

Searching for "What Dwells Within"

"I am what time, circumstance, history have made of me, certainly, but I am also, much more than that.
So are we all."

—James Baldwin

It is my firm belief that everything that happened to me in my youth and early adult years was a stepping-stone on the journey to reconnect with my family, our history, but most importantly, myself.

I was always the quiet member of the family, the middle child, paying attention and listening to everyone around me, but I was too shy and afraid to express my own viewpoints, *my perceptions*. Consequently, I felt left out and was easily persuaded by what I heard and saw, standing silently in the background. This would only confuse me more and augment my already jumbled up memories.

Early on, I was so nice to everyone, trying to be accepted, that if anyone asked me for anything, I just gave it to them. Literally, "even the shirt off my back" if someone had asked for it. I did most of the tough chores in our run-down shack, like getting heavy wood for the stove and drudging bottled water into the house for bathing, drinking, and cleaning. It was pure misery, but it was easy to be taken advantage of because I didn't *talk-back.*

Believe me, as time went on, all this would change. I had to find my own voice and become a leader, not a follower. This allowed my strong personality to come out, but not in a good way—hard-headed, stubborn, doing whatever I felt like doing on a whim and getting into lots of trouble, which in the long run would cause even more pain.

In 2007 when I tried to remember my childhood in Calvert County, I could only recall the times I'd felt utterly lost and alone. I had a mother, a father, brothers and sisters, several cousins, and plenty of friends, but I always felt like I was on the outside looking in because I didn't know how to connect with others. I consciously chose not to do so, letting everyone see the raw, uncontrolled side of me. I just didn't care anymore what people thought of me.

"No person is your friend who demands your silence, or denies your right to grow."

—Alice Walker

I do remember that elementary, middle, and high school came easy to me. Everyone thought I was smart, even my family and especially my mother, but I wanted to be the class clown, laughing on the outside while crying on the inside.

The sheer number of people who came and went in my life did help me to discover small pieces of myself at auspicious stages of development, but the fact remained that I never had anyone around long enough to teach me how to behave and interact with others so I taught myself … or so I thought!

My plan was to experience and mimic things I was attracted to in the lives of my boyfriends, girlfriends, co-workers, and just everyday people you run into while you're stumbling down an uncertain path which leads nowhere. I applied what I observed rather selfishly to benefit myself. I was a loner trapped in a body and mind filled with hurt and confusion, trusting no one.

Ever since I'd met Ms. Valerie at 10 years old (2 x **5** = 10), I was consumed with fear that it wasn't an accident that I was left alone in the burning kitchen of our home as a young child. Did one or all of my family members come to the snap decision with flames rising up around us that they could finally rid themselves of me, the little girl no one seemed to want or love? *The omission,* as I thought of myself.

Of course, I know now that this was unreasonable and caused by the trauma of the fire that scarred my body, but the scars left on my mind, emotions, and self-worth were just as lasting and possibly even more damaging.

It plagued me for years until I took off on my own at the age of 12, becoming a mother at 15 (3 x **5** = 15), leaving Prince Frederick with my dear baby girl, Tonique, as soon as I graduated from high school. Unfortunately, when I left for a brand-new start, I continued to be attracted to the wrong type of men. I was looking for love, but how could I find love when I didn't even know what it was or love myself?

I'm still carrying around the baggage of some personal secrets I wish that I could share that shaped my perceptions on life and people, both positive and negative. Yet, I know things will surface when God knows the time is right because now I'm listening, answering, and reacting. The keyword here is *action!*

God takes care of babies and fools! In my own way, even as a grown woman with children, I was both. In 2008 at 45 years old (another multiple of 5), ROASA, Inc., was my original plan to teach others the strength of Ancestral synergy; something I had never learned. You don't have to tell me that God's hand was leading me. When this idea resonated within me, I had no clue of my own roots.

> **"Can you imagine attempting to educate others about African-American history, but not wanting to know about your own history?"**
>
> —Sharon Parker

Thankfully, as God was preparing me to teach others about notable African-Americans who overcame unsurmountable obstacles and resolved problems that affected every American, He was also giving me the *auspicious gift* to research my own family's history and legacy. *He knew how much I would need these truths for the future, but I didn't!*

In 2010, when my mother died, I was pulled back to Prince Frederick. Almost immediately, unexpected challenges began to auspiciously occur that would open my eyes to see the true synergy of family and community with *dear Amee's* last wish, which she entrusted to me.

I would need to reconnect with the past to express myself in my own voice and find the pathway to the future that I had been separated from for so long.

"Words mean more than what is set down on paper.
It takes the human voice to infuse them
with deeper meaning."

—Maya Angelou

I used to think that God blessed me with the idea for ROASA for other people and their communities, but not for me and the Parker family, nor the rural area of my background in Prince Frederick, Calvert County, Maryland.

I felt I was destined to wander through life disconnected from home and family. I believed it was God's calling for me to help everyone else because my own life, most of which I couldn't remember since the age of 5, had been a roller coaster of pain, joy, near-death experiences, and bad decisions. It was all my own fault. It always had been. Maybe God had chosen to use my faith for others because I was a lost cause?

The decision to do this memoir has forced me to face my past, break through my subconscious blocks, and remember the good, the bad, and the ugly about my family. God allowed me to create the synergistic concept of connecting with one's Ancestors (ROASA) to free me from the bounds that had held me captive for most of my life.

I will have to do everything in my power to share my story to the best of my ability, including the pain and suffering, to accept my true purpose and destiny. This is what I now believe, and I know it will continue to be a lifelong challenge.

"If we are going to be masters of our destiny, we must be masters of the ideas that influence that destiny."

—Dr. John Henrik Clarke

Section III

Hattie Parker's Legacy

Family Ties

Chapter Sixteen

Pathway for the Future

Reflection by Sharon Parker at her mother's funeral:

I'm standing at the graveside watching the interment of my mother, Evelyn M. Parker, feeling like five-year-old Sharon Lee wondering where "Amee" is and why she's not with me.

In my mind, I know she's reunited with God, but in my heart, it's as if I've just opened my eyes, lost and alone, in a strange, derelict house with none of my family with me. All I sense is pain and betrayal.

Where are these feelings coming from? But, a part of me on some other level, recognizes why this emptiness keeps returning to me. I force my consciousness back to the present and look around me. I'm surrounded by Parkers.

Some I know; some I don't know. By the end of this day, I will have met all the Parkers, who may remember me whether I remember them or not. The memories are just beginning to break free from the darkness and shadows.

I learned a little bit about my family history on that solemn day. Mere seeds that God sprinkled upon me to sprout and blossom in my heart that would lead to the pathway that God had planned for me all along, especially since asking that probing question of Him as a timid five-year-old in 1968.

The future was just beginning to assert itself into the tangled web of my memories by opening a small window into the past, not just my own but the history of African-Americans as well. The strands would start to unravel, giving me the hope and confidence to pursue my dreams. *Thank you, God and Amee for showing me the way.*

> **"Maryland had a larger number of free blacks**
> **than any other state in the Union in 1830;**
> **30% of the free blacks lived in Baltimore."**

—Enoch Pratt Library

I don't believe in coincidences; everything happens for a reason given to us by our higher power. People were placed in my life to grant me experiences that I missed growing up.

Shebah Aqeel, who I mentioned in Section I, and her family members Mrs. Ordren Aqeel and Rufus Cannon introduced me to the "African" heritage in my bloodline. Mother Crouch provided me with historical African principles and an old boyfriend in 1998 explained the good and the bad of street "smarts". Patty Earland taught me how to work hard for something you believe in. Brenda Smith and Sharmaine Green showed me the value of friendship. Miss Emma, Virginia E. Hayes Williams, Theresa (Aba) Washington, and so many others supported me throughout this process.

I also became very close to my mother. She shared stories with me of the Parker family and her relationship with my father, the love of her life. It drove her to depression and drink when he helped another family member try to claim her mother Hattie Parker's land.

Please, read the "Acknowledgements" at the end of this book about the wonderful people God put in my life to help me on this difficult journey. These amazing people gave of themselves to lead me on the right path so I could come to know myself.

Each person has a different viewpoint, a unique perception on life—be it Christianity, Islam, other religious faiths; relationships, love, respect for your significant other, and self-respect; street-sense, commonsense, "book sense" as we call it in Calvert County or higher education—all aspects of the spiritual soul.

> **"One's work may be finished someday,**
> **but one's education never!"**

—Alexandre Dumas

Years later I would realize that some people are religious, not spiritual; some are spiritual, not religious; some are merely ethical; and some like myself, are all three. *Aren't we the lucky ones?*

I tend to attract and be drawn to spiritual souls with strong faith and religious ties to the church who believe in justice and equality for all.

How could I ever have survived the rocky path upon which I was originally placed without the gifts of the spirit; belief in fairness and truth; and especially, my Christian upbringing?

The solid faith of the Parker women is what has endured through the generations … from my mother *dear, downtrodden Amee* to my Grandmother Hattie Parker, who died before my birth. The more I learn about my grandmother, the more I feel her spirit living within me, just as I see my mother's glowing smile as she nods her head in approval of me. *Amee* is proud of me; maybe she always was. In the afterlife, I believe my mother knows I'm doing what I was born to do.

It all goes back to me at 5 years old on Adelina Road, the one memory I never lost in all my years of running away— not just from my family; not from Calvert County; not from the people in my life whom I didn't trust, which was just about everyone; but mainly, hiding from my true self.

I had asked an innocent question, and God sent me on a quest that would become my life's journey, not always good and not always bad, but giving me the answers to the tough lessons that would overcome and let me remember what happened to me which had been shrouded in shadows and darkness.

Since I have matured, I don't blame anyone for my mistakes. This process was not by accident. Being rebellious, overly independent from an early age, and determined to find my own way in life, it was *as it should have been ... for me.*

All of this led back to my family, reuniting us which was my mother's final request of me, and the series of events that unearthed my connection to the Parker land which would convince me to step-up and take-charge of my family's property which was in dispute.

"When I Look Back on My Life, I See Pain, Mistakes and Heartache. When I Look in the Mirror, I See Strength, Learned Lessons, and Pride in Myself."

—Anonymous Quote www.chocolatesistergraphics.com

Sharon Parker, self-reflection:

I stand here in the same spot where I stood at 5 years old in 1968, over 50 years ago. The land is within me and I am one with the land, just as "Sharon Lee" and "Sharon Parker" become as "one"—whole and complete.

I asked a question and now I know ... **God heard me** *...*

"God makes three requests of His children:
Do the best you can, where you are,
with what you have now."

—African-American Proverb

Chapter Seventeen

Coming Home and Moving Forward

"Family Must Look Out for Family".

—African-American Proverb

I can look back now and see that "Coming Home" and "Moving Forward" as well as establishing the non-profit organization www.roasalives.org have always been one and the same. *Why did it take me so long to see this with all the auspicious occurrences I'd experienced in my life?*

"The land merged with my ideals, beliefs, and faith."

—Sharon Parker, Owner and President of ROASA, Inc.

Just an inkling of what God had planned for me began to surface in 2003 when I purchased an African-American Ancestral picture for my dear friend, Shebah Aqeel, who had sponsored an event in Brandywine, Maryland. I didn't know at the time why I bought this picture, titled *"Their Beacon is Our Light"*. Shebah, who is now deceased even though I think of her fondly and often, told me to tap into my gift of consciousness. This advice is how Shebah lived her own life.

She told me, "Consciousness is what I am, and what I am is Consciousness." This was the first step on the path of discovery to my heritage.

It would be another 5 years before ROASA, Inc., came to fruition. The previous year, 2007, was when I was birthing the mission statement, goals, and ideals I wanted ROASA to share with individuals, families, and communities. I was 44 years old, just as Barack Obama would become the 44th President of the United States of America.

Sharon, Founder and President of ROASA, Inc., a non-profit organization—company logo

I set up a "100-year timeline" for ROASA, a Video Roadmap to Self, which I use to help others recognize and visualize the synergy that binds their Ancestors, heritage, and history to themselves.

"I am bound to them though I cannot look into their eyes,

or hear their voices.

... I honor their history.

... I cherish their lives.

... I will tell their story.

... I will remember them."

—Unknown Author

My first attempt at writing the "Memoir Original Parker Family" was right after my mother passed away in 2010. I would start and stop many times before God showed me the way and gave me the message that my story of *recovery-to-discovery* must be told ... for my family, for my Ancestors, and for all the other people who needed to find out where they came from and why God placed their souls in unique timelines of heritage. *It has all been done for a purpose and a destiny!*

"When you start about family, about lineage and
ancestry, you are talking about every person on earth."

—Alex Haley

2012 was an auspicious year of success for me. This was the year I met Kirsdi Uunilla, Calvert County Planning and

Zoning Office, who verified the land and my grandmother Hattie Parker's legacy, complete with a picture of The Parker Estate (Chapter Eleven).

Ms. Uunilla also opened up a whole new world to me through the "Maryland Commission on African-American History and Culture." *What would little Sharon Lee from Adelina Road in the small town of Prince Frederick know about African-American history and culture for the state of Maryland and beyond?*

"Let the West have its Technology and Asia its Mysticism! Africa's gift to world culture must be in the realm of Human Relationships."

—Kenneth Kaunda

Since Kirsdi was aware of my interest in her work as an archeologist, tracing the history of slavery in Calvert County, she told me Commissioners were appointed by the Governor of Maryland and managed by the Director of the Frederick Douglas and Benjamin Banneker Museum in Annapolis, Maryland. Formal Director Joni Jones was the name she provided me and asked if I knew her, which I did not. I nodded my head and smiled, never dreaming this prestigious, important work would fall into my hands. Little did I know the *"... large, omnipresent hand of God ..."* had reached out and wrapped my tiny five-year-old fingers securely in His grasp once again.

I had never even heard of the Maryland Commission on African-American History and Culture. What an auspicious, meaningful Commission with strong ties to my own company, ROASA!

I thought, at the very least, I could obtain factual historical information from this Commission to share with my ROASA staff and the young people we were diligently guiding to reach back to their Ancestors for the synergy, integrity, and confidence that would encourage, brighten, and enlighten their souls to promote future professionals. I contacted Director Jones, who invited me to their meetings (every-other-month) and gave me all the State requirements to become a Commissioner. I was completely hooked from the very first meeting I attended!

This gave me the courage to meet with the Chairman of the Commission, Theodore Mack (Ted Mack). Based on his recommendation and if he liked me, my name would be submitted to the Governor's Office, who approved all new Commissioners for the State of Maryland.

Words cannot express how I felt when I received a letter from the Governor of Maryland stating that I was approved and appointed as one of the Commissioners for the Maryland Commission of African-American History and Culture. "Sharon Lee" giggled inside me, and I could hear her childish voice singing, *"I tol' ya' so!"*

I served as Commissioner from 2012-2015. The wealth of African-American knowledge, culture, history, and little known facts that I acquired during this time in my life was priceless. Only God could have made this happen for me as I sat among scholars and historians at the front table— *"Sharon Lee had finally made it to the adult table, and she was growing up proud and strong!"*—at every Commissioners' public meeting, which were held all over the state of Maryland.

The Unveiling of the 1865 Maryland State-wide Quilt that includes Sharon's Ancestor's House—The Parker Family Estate on Adelina Road, Prince Frederick, MD.

One key task that I will never forget was the creation of a Statewide Emancipation 1865 quilt. This included telling the story of all 23 counties in Maryland (*you got it, 2+3=5!*) and the separate Municipal City of Baltimore through pictures, quotes, people, actual items, and the celebration of each county freeing Maryland slaves in 1865. This was a new venue for me. I had to use my voice, my creativity, and learn to research that which I had been hiding from all my life.

Of course, I was assigned to investigate the story of my own hometown and Calvert County. I take every assignment I've ever been given very seriously, and this challenge was no exception. Not even sure where these feelings were coming from deep inside me, I wanted to assure that my own family, the Original Parker Family of Adelina Road, would have a place in history forever. That's right, the center square of the quilt for all of Maryland to see is Benjamin and Grace Parker, Jr. and The Parker Estate of Calvert County. How was I to know when Kirsdi Uunilla gave me the picture of our family home, confirmed by my Aunt Elizabeth, that it would be with 22 other squares and Baltimore City equaling 24 to make one large Maryland Statewide Quilt showing the Emancipation of African-Americans families in 1865? "***Yes, indeed, Priceless!***"

The Maryland State Emancipation Quilt is housed at The Wiley H. Bates Legacy Center, 1101 Smithville Street, Annapolis, MD 21401. When the Commission has its meetings, it reverently travels and is displayed in a different county or city in Maryland. We share the wealth of beauty!

"Sad will be the day when the American people forget their traditions and their history, and no longer remember that the country they love, the institutions they cherish, and the freedom they hope to preserve, were born from the throes of armed resistance to tyranny, and nursed in the rugged arms of fearless men."

—Roger Sherman

The success and growth I experienced through 2012-2015 was God's way of preparing me for the interactions I would have with people, my past, and my destiny. I was healing myself as well as the people around me who were suffering in silence, just as I had done for over forty years of my life!

"Success is to be measured not so much by the position that one has reached in life as by the obstacles which he has to overcome while trying to succeed."

—Booker T. Washington

But with each success, a little rain must fall. In 2013 (at age 50, **5** x 10), me and my siblings would be shocked yet brought together in unity, as dear *Amee* had wished, when the truth of The Parker Family Estate was finally revealed.

I would also come to know how closely God has been watching over me. I have almost died three times in my life: from the fire in 1968 at 5 years old (Chapter Six); in a car accident at age 17; and again, at age 20. These last two incidents will be addressed in the sequel to this memoir. In each instance, my dreams alerted me and angels protected me so that I could make a full recovery, despite the odds.

I am thankful for my many blessings. I realize now why I was chosen by God to speak for my Ancestors' land and Hattie Parker's legacy as they look down upon me from heaven and whisper softly in my soul that there is unfinished business to handle on earth.

"Closing my eyes to connect with my roots I sense the wisdom of my ancestors. And my grandmother smiles."

—Kira, The Gossamer Path

Chapter Eighteen

Who's Who ... The Original Parkers

"Family History ... Who am I?
... I am the conclusion of my Ancestors' story.
... I am the prologue to my descendants' story."

—Anonymous Author

In Section I, Chapters Eleven and Twelve, I revealed the long, drawn out legal status of my grandmother Hattie Parker's legacy concerning the land, particularly the one-acre plot where the large, beautiful Parker Estate had once stood. This was the house I lived in with my mother and siblings until the fire in the kitchen of 1968—the home of my birth and my birthright, which for most of my life I couldn't remember.

With my auspicious increments of the number 5 in 2013, at 50 years of age, I finally took notice of the gossip and stories that I had turned a deaf ear to all my life. God was bringing me back to the land, and this time I was forced to listen because the descendants of Hattie Parker, which of course included me and my siblings, were being sued by a family member for ownership of this prime one-acre of land that had direct access to Adelina Road, including the utilities, and other 5-to-6-acre plots of the entire Estate split up for the four children (Hattie Parker, Isabelle Saunders, Mary Boyd, and Benjamin Parker, III) of Benjamin and Grace Parker, Jr., legal original owners per Calvert County records show Benjamin Parker, Sr. This is an error (Chapter Twelve).

My oldest brother Leo, my younger sister Lynn, and I had paid taxes for a three-year period in arrears on this one-acre of property earlier in 2013 to keep it from being sold in a tax auction, thanks to my Aunt Elizabeth (Hattie Parker's daughter, only living sibling) for seeing the announcement of the sale in the newspaper. On Christmas eve, we received a certified letter from a lawyer claiming a Parker cousin had a legal deed to this land, and we would have to reclaim it in this lawsuit against the descendants of Hattie Parker if we did not sign a plat that approved for residential via residue.

I want to briefly reiterate my sincere thanks to Kirsdi Uunilla of the Calvert County Planning and Zoning Office who helped me find the Original Parker Estate location and a picture of the house in June 2012, and Ms. Margaret Phipps of the Register of Wills for Calvert County, who in

December 2013 gave me copies of the original Wills of my great-grandparents referred to as Benjamin and Grace Parker, Sr., not Jr., and established me as their Personal Representative (PR), since they were no longer living.

I had been vaguely aware that my mother and Aunt Elizabeth had filed suits to reclaim this land in both 1985 and 2007. I had been given paperwork by my oldest sister Patty a few days before my mother's funeral, which I never really looked at, but kept in a safe place. On the same day that I met with Ms. Phipps, I learned that these two lawsuits had never been filed. The land was calling to me and my sense of fairness and justice was enraged. I became the family spokesperson.

"Hold onto to your hat! Who's Who in The Original Parker Family is full of surprises. Some unexpected characters had not yet come to light in 2013!"

—Sharon Parker

"As you know, in this country Anglo-Americans are 75 to 76 percent home ownership in this country, where Hispanics and African-Americans are less than 50 percent."

—Alfonso Jackson

Even in a small town where everybody knows everybody, identity theft can occur. Benjamin Parker, Jr. was married to Grace Parker, referred to as "Gracie". His son, Benjamin, III married Violet Hurley. "The Plaintiff" in the case against the descendants of Hattie Parker was from this family line. The Plaintiff never married, the name remaining "Parker".

Aunt Elizabeth, Hattie Parker's daughter, remembers The Plaintiff going from house to house, family to family, asking them to sign a legal paper for "water rights" to the Parker Estate. In this timeframe, many of the African-Americans could not read well so many signed it based on faith from someone they had known all their lives. Aunt Elizabeth recalls that, "I didn't sign it 'cause it just didn't look right."

The legal paper was in actuality an authorization to deed this one-acre of land to The Plaintiff, claiming to be soul heir to the property. Even The Plaintiff's own family members weren't aware of this duplicity. This fraudulent deed of ownership was accepted many times in Calvert County.

In a written disposition, however, under oath the truth had to be told. This disposition would be brought before Judge Clackett, who was presiding over the case for Judge Cal Stewart who had previously endorsed the erroneous deed.

Clackett ruled in favor of the Defendants: my Aunt Mary Elizabeth Parker-Willet, myself, and my siblings as Hattie Parker's heirs, the rightful owners of this land.

This is just the beginning, but a battle well-earned and deserved for my Grandmother's legacy. The story will continue in the sequel to this memoir after the property has been zoned and a new deed prepared.

A sad realization surfaced during my research into the family. I finally understood why my mother was so upset whenever she walked by this plot of land and the fact that The Plaintiff had my mother's and grandmother's house torn down. The Plaintiff was first cousin to my father, Wilford Hurley, and he aided her in misrepresenting her identity. This devastated my mother's emotional and physical health, leading to her excessive drinking and, eventually, her death.

So as in all things in life bestowed by God, we take the good and the bad, remembering our family with bittersweet feelings of love and acceptance of who we are and the synergy of us all from our Ancestral roots.

"Don't look now, there are more surprises in the past!"

—Sharon Parker

Chapter Nineteen

Aunt Elizabeth Shares Her Stories

"The way to right wrongs is to turn
the light of truth upon them."

—Ida B. Wells-Barnett

I want to introduce you to my Aunt Elizabeth. At 92 years old, she's a ball of fire with a memory like a steel trap. *She doesn't miss a trick or forget anything!* That, of course, is wonderful, but sometimes…?

Never mind that, she always tells her stories with truth, love, and forgiveness. She's been keeping *us kids* straight all our lives. She was a dear sister and so helpful to my mother in her time of sorrow and need.

Aunt Elizabeth was also very close to her mother, my Grandmother Hattie Parker—*"May she rest in peace,"*—as my generation of Parkers takes care of her land and legacy.

I love the grandmother I never knew more each day as I learned the pillar Hattie was in the community. She is sending me synergy from heaven to instill in others the importance of knowing our family ties and Ancestral history.

I believe the spirit of my grandmother, Hattie Parker, and my mother, Evelyn M. Parker, and family stories of fun, faith, and failure—*"gittin' back up and tryin' ag'in til' ya' get it right!"*—are what initially planted the idea in my hardhead that would become ROASA, *"Remembering Our Ancestors Synergistic Association, Inc."*

By the end of this chapter, Aunt Elizabeth will seem like your Aunt too. She enriches the lives of everyone around her. I may have become the family "voice" in legal matters, but there's no doubt that Aunt Elizabeth is the family Matriarch. "She's never met a stranger" and knows everybody on Adelina Road and in Prince Frederick. The knowledge and wisdom she shares with a heart as big as the ocean brings comfort and joy to everyone around her. And she does so love to tell her stories and laugh, laugh, laugh!

"The true worth of a race must be measured by the character of its womanhood ..."

—Mary McLeod Bethune

"One of the lessons that I grew up with was to always stay true to yourself and never let what somebody says distract you from your goals."

—Michelle Obama

This quote by former First Lady Michelle Obama reminds me of the values that were instilled in me by my family. Somehow, I begrudgingly accepted these sacred truths within me, though I certainly would never have admitted it at the time, nor did I even realize it!

2015 Sharon with First Lady, Michelle Obama, in Wash. DC

Talk about auspicious occurrences, this one is probably at the top of the list! It happened very recently—this year,

2017, in fact, during the writing of this memoir. I drove out to Calvert County to talk to Aunt Elizabeth about my Grandmother Hattie Parker after a comment was made that I was so much like her.

I didn't want to miss one little detail of these family stories, many of which happened before my birth. I called a member of my support team, whom I know is a copious notetaker, and talked to my Aunt on speaker phone to collaborate these precious moments in time.

Aunt Elizabeth started off by saying that everyone came to the Parker House to "… feed 'em … that's what they came for…" The estate was surrounded by vegetable gardens so my mother didn't just lose her mother Hattie's home, but she lost the gardens that fed her nine children when the property was squatted upon by The Plaintiff.

Stories came out that day that shocked and then delighted me. What a whirlwind of feelings! The Parker Estate had a room in the back that was used to "lay out the body" when an African-American died in Prince Frederick because there was no funeral home for "our people." There was a black undertaker that "lived down the hill," but the Parker women would clean and dress the body, sitting in reverence and respect for the departed. The services were held in this room on the Parker Estate. The Parker commitment to the land and the people was amazing!

When Aunt Elizabeth started talking about The Plaintiff, I experienced a sadness that overwhelmed me. It seems the fire in the kitchen was *not* an accident!

A young man (late teens to early twenties) named Earl who had been a guest in our home and was raised as a foster son by a friend of The Plaintiff's named Ms. Bungie was hired by someone whose name will not be mentioned; she will be known as "that same person" who started this fire. After our family moved into the trailer owned by one of our cousins, which I mentioned in Chapter Four, there was a shed behind the trailer where my mother kept all the keepsakes and important papers that she'd removed from our home. Earl was also hired or coerced by that same person to burn this structure as well.

Aunt Elizabeth saw the fire from Adelina Road and ran down to get us out of the trailer before we were injured. The quick action on my Aunt's part saved the trailer from catching fire. We moved out soon afterward, but all Deeds, Bills, and legal paperwork showing ownership of the property and house by my mother and her sister was destroyed as well as family mementoes that can never be replaced.

We believe that it was that same person who hired a white man, Bobby Bucker, to "… knock down the house …" as my mother used to cry and say over and over again. I can't help but be shocked by the mean-spirited vindictiveness of this cousin. I'm sure there's more to the story than we will ever know.

The tone of the conversation with Aunt Elizabeth turned to sunshine as she started talking about someone she called *"Pie; that's what everybody called him."*

"Wait, wait, Aunt Elizabeth! Who was *Pie?"* I asked.

"Why, he was Benjamin Parker, Sr.'s father [Aunt Elizabeth knew Benjamin, Jr. as Sr. because of the records] also named Benjamin. He owned the land and built the house."

I was flabbergasted! Another Benjamin Parker? Aunt Elizabeth went on to tell me that he had a prosperous tobacco farm, went to Baltimore to sell his crop, hired many workers in Prince Frederick. In other words, Great-Great-Grandfather Benjamin was an entrepreneur!

And remarkably, the *real* Benjamin, Sr.'s granddaughter, Hattie Parker, was an entrepreneur as well. She also went to Baltimore and did business on a high-level, including taking care of financial affairs and establishing loans in her own name, which was unheard-of for women—all women, but especially African-American women—two generations before my own. The business/entrepreneur gene seems to have passed down through the Parker family line every other generation. But that need not be the case anymore. I am so proud that this opportunity has been blessed upon my daughters and will be available for my grandchildren.

Things have come full circle in my family as I researched "Benjamin Parker, Sr." He was born a freeman of color in 1828 in Prince Frederick, Maryland, where his roots *seem* to be entrenched perhaps as early as the 17th century. There is more research to be done to find out how far our family goes back in Calvert County, possibly all the way to 1654 when the town was established as a predominantly African-American Colony of free landowners.

There will definitely be more about Benjamin "Pie" Parker, Sr.—*"God love 'im!"* Sharon says with a chuckle and the smile that lights up her face so like the one that adorns Aunt

Elizabeth's grin—and the Parker legacy in the next book of this family saga.

"Bless you and thank you, Aunt Elizabeth, Grandmother Hattie Parker, and my mother, Evelyn Parker, for being The Parker Family Matriarchs!"

—Sharon Parker

"But what of Black women? I most sincerely doubt if any other race of women could have brought its fineness up through so devilish a fire!"

—W. E. B. DuBois

Section IV

"Leading WithIN!"

Auspicious 5th Conference

ROASA, Inc., Annual Event

Chapter Twenty

One More Auspicious Occurrence!

"There is no greater gift you can give or receive than to honor your calling. It's why you were born."

—Oprah Winfrey

I have shared quite a few *auspicious occurrences* from my life in this memoir, but I have only scratched the surface with the magnitude of messages, gifts, and blessings that have been put in my path since I was a lonely little five-year-old.

I'll be the first to admit that I had to be reminded repeatedly by my Heavenly Father of my *"calling"* with the stubborn certainty engrained in me that I could handle everything just fine on my own, even when headed in the wrong direction.

As you know by reading my story, it took over four decades for me to stop fighting, ignoring, and hiding from the truth within me. Hardheaded doesn't even begin to describe my temperament. But that which makes us pigheaded and stubborn also makes us strong and determined with an action-oriented mindset … once we get on the right path!

"What we learn as children
will follow us the rest of our lives."

—Sharon Parker

So, bear with me just a moment longer, I have *"one more auspicious occurrence"* to share with you. Once I opened the doors and windows to my inner self, letting in the light of divinity and connecting with the synergy and integrity of my Ancestors, beautiful momentous occasions began popping out all over the place in every aspect of my life. In the words of my new mentor:

"Open up to new possibilities!
Inquiry, curiosity and discovery can occur
when we put aside the knowledge
that the possibility door can open up!"

—Sandra Yancey, Award-winning Entrepreneur
CEO & Founder of eWomenNetwork

Let me just say, I wasn't even supposed to be at this event. I had heard of Sandra Yancey, the speaker, but had never met her. It had been a last-minute decision because I needed to meet with the couple who had invited me to the function afterwards, but other powers were at work that none of us knew about.

I slipped into the room a few minutes late, taking an empty seat surrounded by over 100 people, most of whom were total strangers. I sat there listening for quite some time, absorbing everything, when suddenly that old feeling of "Sharon Parker" becoming silent, introverted "Sharon Lee" stole over me. I screamed within, *"Not this time!"*

I quietly raised my hand to ask a question.

"When the things that stop you show up, say to yourself, "I'm not going there," and stay focused on your dream!"

—Sandra Yancey

Little did I know that I would end up becoming part of the presentation, engaged in a direct conversation with the speaker who unknowingly guided me through the breakthrough of reality that will keep me focused on the mission of www.roasalives.org and www.leadingwithin.org

I learned that day that I am not alone, and many "Sharon Parkers" have little "Sharon Lees" in their memories to overcome. These people thanked me for speaking up!

"We will break through the barriers that steal our Voices! We all shall reach down deep and Lead from WithIN!"

—Sharon Parker

I can't begin to tell you the big smile that glows on my face with pride as I see all my hard work coming together for other souls trapped within themselves. All it takes is believing in yourself, caring about others, and tapping into your God-given gifts!

"Life's most persistent and urgent question is,
'What are you doing for others?'"

—Dr. Martin Luther King, Jr.

Sandra Yancey and Sharon Parker

Chapter Twenty-One

The Power of Synergy and
My Auspicious Number 5!

"We are so much more than the sum of our parts.
We are added, subtracted, multiplied, divided
in infinite variations. We are created again with every
thought, experience, memory, and emotion.
That equation takes more than a mind to understand.
It takes a heart and soul—Synergy!"

—Printable Quotes by *Shala*

Anyone who picks up this memoir and even just skims these words will see my **auspicious number 5** highlighted throughout the pages. I hope it will draw you into my story so you too can remember yourself at 5 years old. Where were you headed? Where did you end up? This is my equation; this is my heart and soul; this is my **Synergy!**

For decades, it was my first and only memory at age 5 in 1968, standing on a narrow country road in Prince Frederick,

Maryland. It repelled me, yet compelled me. I clung to it all my life, not sure why, but it would eventually bring me back to my family, creating the mission for my company, opened on the auspicious birthday of Rosa Parks, "Remembering Our Ancestors Synergistic Association, Inc.," (ROASA) www.roasalives.org

This year with the ***auspicious 5th anniversary*** of ROASA's Annual Unconditional Love Retreat, I am excited to share my memoir ***"True Synergy Works…Leading Within, Seven (7) Defining Principles of Knowing Self to Birth Greatness!"*** ROASA's Leading WithIN! Conference has been birthed out of my auspicious journey for all to see www.leadingwithin.org

"I truly believe in positive synergy,
that your positive mindset gives you a more hopeful
outlook and belief that you can do something great,
you will do something great!"

—Russell Wilson

ROASA, Inc., is a not-for-profit organization which serves as an all-inclusive platform of structured workshops, community outreach events, and business-to-youth who can connect and *re*-connect through synergy with inspiring professionals and would-be professionals who seek the value in a mindset that builds true business-to-business relationships, strong collaborations, and long-term beneficial partnerships. Our promotional hashtags are #TrueSynergyWorks2K17 and #RLWC2K17.

As Sharon Parker, Founder and CEO of "Remembering Our Ancestors Synergistic Association" since 2008, we offer a diverse and inclusive platform to transcend generations of professionals and individuals who want to meet, learn, grow, and establish businesses, corporations, and non-profit organizations using the ideals and integrity of our Ancestors, our roots, to promote ourselves as the entrepreneurs and leaders of the future, which we will, in turn, pass onto the blossoming young adults, *the millennials,* who will carry this synergistic movement onward and upward!

Our signature programs such as ROASA Youth Empowerment Series (RYES), pronounced "Rise"; ROASA's Ancestral Sighting; ROASA's Unconditional Love Café that was just launched in my hometown of Calvert County on February 11, 2017; and ROASA's Roadmap to Self-Workshop will serve to bring true synergy to all we touch.

ROASA's Youth Empowerment Series, pronounced "Rise"
Program established in 2012

"Coming together is the beginning.
Keeping together is progress.
Working together is success."

—Henry Ford

We will all share our own 5-year stories to uncover the ideals, goals, dreams, and leadership abilities which have been buried too long beneath the pressure of day-to-day stress. There is a new road ahead of you, a pathway to lead you out of the hustle-and bustle of "overwhelm" and the darkness and shadows of fear and lack of self-worth.

"You can make a difference once you reach within to accept the courage, confidence, and joy inside of you!"

—Sharon Parker, author, speaker, entrepreneur, mentor

Our targeted audience for this *auspiciously wonderful 5th* ROASA, Inc., event is for all ages, stages, and walks-of-life:

industry; government; merchants; clergy and non-profits; youth leaders; college and high school students; and anyone, ***absolutely everyone***, who is ready to tear open the boxes we sealed within ourselves that contain what we perceived as our shortcomings and failures—the things we never wanted anyone else to see.

Most times, however, it is the setbacks in life that we learn the most from. When the contents of these boxes spill forth and we share the hard lessons-learned, we find that "we are not alone." There are others who have been on the same self-limiting, self-defeating journey. We'll never forget these troubled failures, but we'll never repeat them, either. It's time to release them and move on!

Fragmented family stories, self-conscious traits, and ridicule, when we fight back, can turn stubbornness, lonely independence, and raw sense of self into determination, strength of character, and the belief that we can do anything, achieve anything, and create everything!

Believe me, I know of what I speak ... as you've read my memoir, you've seen me fight this transition; ignore the callings of my faith, beliefs, truth, and ethics; and finally, not give up, but *give in and cherish* the blessings around me that have made me whole and complete as an individual.

I know that my journey from *recovery-to-discovery* is not complete ... will never be complete ... I accept each day as a challenge and a chance to grow, heal, believe, and share my experiences with others who need to ***"... reach out and touch the hand of God ... your higher power ..."*** even if it's the hand of the soul vessel standing right in front of you, an angel placed in your path from your true Maker and Superior Being.

I'm here to tell you, ***"You can do this!"*** I hope and pray it doesn't take you as long as it did hardheaded little "Sharon Lee" to overcome myself, ***find*** my true self and get to the "Destiny and Fulfillment*: Recovery-to-Discovery."*

"There is such unparalleled joy, excitement, and exuberance from letting go of the lingering past! I want to share this feeling of freedom by giving love and acceptance to everyone I reach, touch, and release from the darkness and fear that was my life for far too long!"

—Sharon Parker/Sharon Lee, one and the same.

We are honored and blessed to have as our keynote speaker at the 5th ROASA's Leading WithIN Conference, Reverend Dr. Barbara Reynolds, author of the late Coretta Scott King's new book, "My Life, My Love, My Legacy." We couldn't ask for a more perfect advisor and mentor than Dr. Barbara Reynolds, talented author, newswoman, commentator, and spiritual leader. She will take us down the pathway which I challenge each and every one of you to share together with us in June 2017. This auspicious 5th ROASA Conference is destined for greatness, acceptance, and true evolution!

"Synergy—the bonus that is achieved when things work together harmoniously!"

"Don't be left behind by your own stubbornness!"

—Sharon Parker, reflecting on her personal Transition

Chapter Twenty-Two

Honoring the First Unconditional Love Retreat from 2013

"If your actions inspire others to dream more, learn more, do more and become more, you are a leader."

—John Quincey Adams

"As I pause in reflection on this first section of my ongoing journey, knowing there is so much more to come, I update my concept of Synergy as: 'The energy which God uses to connect us with our Ancestors to bring His people together for the benefit of helping those with less.' I have been so blessed and wish to shine the light on those who uplift others with their stories of triumph!"

—Sharon Parker, in gracious humility

The board members at ROASA, Inc., Sharmaine Green, Brenda Smith and myself, Sharon Parker, truly thank all the great community leaders, youth activists, pastors, executive directors, career counselors, RYES's youth, unsung heroes, and wise elders who came out to ROASA's first Annual Unconditional Love Retreat that was held in 2013, *auspiciously* 2017 is our 5th anniversary.

Here are a few reflections shared by thriving business women who attended the very first ROASA, Inc, Unconditional Love Retreat:

Barbara Talley: "On May 17-18th, 2013, I had the privilege of serving as Co-MC and participating in ROASA's "1st Annual Unconditional Love Retreat." So much happened that it is almost impossible to put into words, but I would like to attempt to share my sentiments and observations for those who missed the event.

"Firstly, the speaker lineup was powerful. Over the course of the two days, we were addressed by dozens of women who have faced struggles, triumphed over them, and then showed up to share the secrets of how to overcome any adversity. Participants were taken on an emotional rollercoaster ride, brought to tears by survivors of addictions, abuse, rape, incest, and other childhood traumas, to rolling on the floor in laughter with the infectious humor of Sylvia Traymore Morrison.

"Secondly, the elders (several in their eighties and nineties) lovingly yet forcefully called us to commit to a deeper level of responsibility and service to save and uplift our young folk, our families, and ourselves.

Thirdly, I have to mention the connections that were made between entrepreneurs and employees; between old and young; between high school educated to those with multiple Ph.D.'s; and between dreamers and those looking for someone to encourage them to not only reach their dreams, but more importantly that have a duty to fulfill their dreams.

"In closing, I'll just say it was an eye-opener for some and life-changing for others, but no one left without something as each was personally touched in a different way. Sharon Parker's goal was fulfilled as she brought together this diversity, number, and caliber of speakers to not only encourage each other, but to collaborate and multiply their influence as we jointly seek to raise awareness, empower our young, and gain financial freedom."

A message to our community back in 2013: "Sharon Parker's goal was fulfilled as she brought together this diversity, number, and caliber of speakers to not only encourage each other, but to collaborate and multiply their influence as we jointly seek to raise awareness, empower our young, and gain financial freedom. P.S. The first day was so impactful that I brought a friend the next day. This is what she had to say about the event:"

"It never ceases to amaze me how the universe provides one with the very exact thing they need at the very exact time they need it. I am in the process of evolving and healing, and this weekend I found myself amongst other women on a pilgrimage to greatness. We stood before each other broken and yearning to fill ourselves with love and light. What we experienced was unconditional love. We laughed, we cried, we shared, we sang, and we came together and found strength to continue evolving and to make a difference in our lives and the lives we touch. I can't wait until next year!!"

Dr. E. A. Beth Sears: "I was honored and awed by the opportunity to interact with such accomplished women at the first annual ROASA conference. In addition to the company of such accomplished people, I was especially moved by their stories of their journeys. Success takes hard work, and these individuals had many barriers, which would have thwarted the journey of many, but chose to persevere and use their stories as inspiration to others.

"By listening to one another and acknowledging a person's brilliance and gifts, we can move a long way toward breaking down barriers that keep us apart. Many thanks for the gift of the first annual ROASA conference as my life was enriched by it."—Beth

Lisa Dove Washington: "My experience at the ROASA's 1st Annual Women's Unconditional Love Retreat was absolutely amazing. I learned so much about who I am through my experience at this wonderful retreat. The energy that generated in the room was breathtaking and if you missed this experience you missed something very precious. I learned about sisterhood, my ancestry, and about unconditional love. The retreat was a weekend of listening and sharing and where our elders took us under their wings and showed us how to open our hearts, minds, and should do so to others.

"I can't wait to do this all over again next year. I learned more in those 48 hours than I have learned in a long time. I am so grateful for the opportunity to have witnessed such an event and the knowledge that I gained was priceless.

"This retreat will gain more power than any of us can imagine and I can't wait to share that I was there first. I was honored to speak at this retreat and look forward to having the chance to do it all over again in 2014!"

Tanya McMillian: "ROASA's 1st Annual Women's Retreat in Washington, DC, was an extraordinary experience for me. When Sharon invited me to be a speaker, I had no idea I would be impacted the way I was at the event. I learned so much from other speakers about history and life itself. The young women that were encouraged to attend and benefit from the sessions were not the only ones able to take away crucial information that would prove to change the life of every listener in the room.

"Sharon knew what she was doing when she invited successful businesswomen with diverse backgrounds because each person was able to extend a piece of themselves to someone at the event. Participants and speakers could grow while having their spirit fed with vital historical and current life stories. What a fantastic women's retreat!!!"

Diane Tuckman: "It was quiet at my exhibitor table so I was quickly drawn to attend the sessions. Each speaker was more engaging than the previous one! I learned so much about the challenges faced by one and all and how they creatively and by their strength changed their lives and the lives of their families. And to think that I have challenges… just listen to these amazing women! The leaders from the older generation were most inspiring.

"I came as an exhibitor and an observer. I left with a greater insight into the wonderful works done by POWER women who do dynamic work within their community and beyond. Indeed, working with the new generation is so important."

Abena Disroe: "I want to thank you wholeheartedly for inviting me to be one of your speakers at the wonderful retreat. The energy, warmth, down-to-earthiness, and vitality of the speakers were very special. I say it was special because the circle of these powerful women gave me the courage to share my story, which before this weekend "I HAD NEVER" shared my story that was attached to painful memories. I now have the strength and courage to move forward with that half-done manuscript to completion. I WILL complete it, as I am compelled to share the whole story to give the inspiration, hope, and courage to others that

I found at the ROASA, Inc. retreat. I thank all the powerful speakers, not for only what they communicated, but for the moments off the camera and film where they embraced me with sisterhood, unconditional Love, and encouragement.

"I know that I have been anointed to minister to the youth, and the elder ROASA members have given me that extra confidence that I needed to move forward, not only for myself but for the empowerment of others. The rape and the abuse somehow seems so minor to the purpose in life that it has shown me, and the validation that ROASA has given me to continue the empowerment of others because you, Ms. Abena, you have the gift, and I will always use it for the upliftment of others. Thank you ROASA!"

Gail Crowder: "My experience from the ROASA event was an absolutely enriching one. Sharing the same space with dynamic women who helped shaped the African American experience was a delight. As a speaker, I prepared to pour into the lives of the attendees; however, the phenomenal women in attendance as well as the other speakers of the event poured into my life in a very significant way.

Events like the ROASA, Inc., event are important due to the impact they have on our priorities. As I deal with the opportunities of life and manage all that is before me, I was reminded of the importance to stop, reflect, and remember all that has been done in order for me to do what I am privileged to do today and more importantly remind my children of the same."

"If you want the cooperation of humans around you, you make them feel THEY ARE IMPORTANT and you do that by being genuine and humble."

—Nelson Mandela

Chapter Twenty-Three

My Farewell Message ... for now ...
With My Auspicious 2 + 3 = 5!

"Everyone has dreams and goals. The only difference between a goal and a dream is a goal IS a dream with—ACTION!"

—John Chow

As the Founder of "Remembering Our Ancestors Synergistic Association (ROASA)," Inc. www.roasalives.org and now www.leadingwithin.org as well, both not-for-profit organizations to help people realize their dreams and goals, I thought long and hard about how to end this first volume of my personal and family Memoir. I was humbled and choked up with emotion by the amazing words written in 2013 after our very first ROASA Unconditional Love Retreat. And the successive years have been just as powerful! How can anyone follow the unbelievable outpouring of souls stripped to their bare essence for the evolution, recovery, discovery, and pure love of others?

There is no doubt that a second or even third volume is essential for this Memoir because in many ways the dreams that have become goals through "ACTION!" are continuously and *auspiciously* beginning with each new day.

I believe this is true of everyone if you but open your eyes to see; open your ears to hear; open your heart to care about and love humanity; and open your soul to *know* the profound messages, gifts, and inner reflections from God or whomever you consider your higher power. ***These are the dreams and goals that we are all manifesting if we but pay attention!***

My story is told through the eyes, ears, fears, and tears of five-year-old "Sharon Lee" who grew up to become me, Entrepreneur "Sharon Parker". As I read back over these pages, I can't believe what has transpired during the years which dwindled down to months in the writing of this book, and my life? I'm blown away when I look back from where I have come from, but even more startled by where I'm headed, now that I have allowed myself to not only touch, but reach out and cling to with all my strength ***"... the mighty hand of God ..."***

"The joy, enthusiasm, excitement, and achievements have far outweighed the trauma, sorrow, terror, and anxiety that made a quiet, scared little five-year-old run away and hide within herself, hide from the world, hide from everything... But it has so been worth it!"

—Sharon Parker, aka Sharon Lee

"Every great dream begins with a dreamer. Always remember you have within you the Strength, the Patience, and the Passion to reach for the stars and change the world."

—Harriet Tubman

Acknowledgements

MY
FAMILY
AND
FRIENDS!

When you discover and ultimately accept your destiny, it becomes effortless to recognize those that God has placed on your pathway to assure that you achieve His divine purpose, which He has entrusted to your soul's journey.

Personally, I strongly believe that it has always been His design and purpose for me, and I am finally listening to those jewels of messages, gifts, and visions that He placed right in front of me in plain sight. No matter the successes or failures, those whom God has brought before me will forever leave a lasting impression on my life, and I will share them and what they have taught me with the world!

It's an honor to personally thank my family and friends for their contributions, knowledge, and memories which inspired me to write this book.

Those close to me know that I have found it very difficult to express what I wanted to share about my life and my family. Countless streams of emotions and memories were repressed/suppressed in my mind, even though they were sometimes recalled in my dreams.

After spending four decades stuck in my own way, I decided to find the willpower to share my life's story in the hope that it could transform the lives of other five-year-old girls that may be stuck in a grown woman's body. Too often caring and confident women get trapped in their minds and find it hard to release that scared five-year-old little girl that still lives within.

To my Remembering our Ancestors Synergistic Association (ROASA), Inc., tribe, your names will forever define the meaning *"True Synergy Works...Leading Within!"*

The word "Synergy" is a word that I do not take lightly, which is why I used it for my company ROASA and in the title of my Memoir. I have embraced and lived by this word as it has served to guide phenomenal individuals to me who work tirelessly to inspire young people, adults, and elders with their stories of joy and triumphs.

This is a personal *"Thank You"* for your efforts in supporting your community through ROASA, Inc., and being a much-needed part of my personal journey. I am forever grateful for the powerful and inspirational messages and support from:

Hattie N. Washington, Pastor Mary L. Wilson, Dr. Barbara Reynolds, Commissioner Barbara Dunn, Peggy Hightower, Dr. Beth Sears, Ph.D., Theresa (Aba) Washington, Mother Ordren Aqeel, Renee Robinson, Tattiana Aqeel, Kailasa Aqeel, Andrew Goode, Miss Emma Ward, Pastor Yasmine Bell-Flemons, Senior Pastor Tony Flemons, Sandra Craft, Lydia Mason-Gladden, Gail Crowder, Tawawn Lowe, Lisa Dove Washington, Sylvia Traymore Morrison, Dr. E. Faye Williams, Juanita BusyBee Britton, Mother Janice Crouch, Frances Luckett-Hunter, Pastor Reginald Luckett, Joan Braitsch, Pastor Denise McDowell, Janelle Bruce, Shalonda Holt, Monica Clark, Kimberly Taylor, Cynthia Lane, Elizabeth Lane, Catherine Thomas, Eileen Cook, Darrick Johnson, Lamont Carey, Dr. Leslie LaVonne, Wendy Carter, Sandra Jeanette Wright, Sir Charles Cary, Rudolph A. Coleman, Sheila Hinds, Joseph Sealey, Robert Garrett, Larry White, Sr., Alyscia Cunningham, Marshall Cunningham,

Brenda Smith, Stacy Cunningham, Henry Jones, Seldom Brown (Skip), Joan Thompson, Janice Armstrong (DrJai), Yin Chang, Rodney Gray, Chi Chi, Cheriss May, Garrett Mays, Ray Winbush, Mary Bazargan, Mary Taylor, Robin Finnell, Carolyn White-Washington, Chernelle Luckey, Tonique Parker, Shawan Dawkins, Wakeelah Cannon, Latifah Cannon, Curtis King, Valerie Hampton, Terri Reaves, Claude Parren, Savyon Frith, Trevon Frith, Shawn Parker, Kevin Parker, Randi Parker, Tyesha Parker, Dana Parker, Michele Hammond, Dr. Peggy Valentine (RIP), my Capital Speaking Club sisters, American Mothers, Inc. sisters, Robert C. Weaver—Blacks in Government sisters and brothers, and DC Boxing and Wrestling sisters and brothers, and other community sisters and brothers that played a part in my *#Roadmap*.

Thanks again to each of you identified on the Dedication Page at the front of this book for you have been chosen to take this journey along with me, beside me every step of the way.

Blessings to You All,
Sharon Parker, writing as "Sharon Lee"

Sharon Parker Biography

by Stephanie Manns

"The impulse to dream had been slowly beaten out of me by experience. Now it surged up again and I hungered for books, new ways, of looking and seeing."

—Richard Wright

Sharon Parker is many things to many people, a legacy seeker, a passionate and purposed teacher, a National Community Connector, and a heart-led historian.

But really ... she is just a woman on a mission to capture the stories of African-American heroes—the celebrated and unsung—and to share them with the world, 365 days a year.

When she left her hometown of Calvert County, Maryland, as a young woman to chase her dreams, Sharon had no idea where that road would lead. The journey would take her to the Department of Housing and Urban Development (HUD) as a Federal Public Servant for 30 years, which birthed her passion to serve her community, and to the Maryland Commission on African-American History and Culture (MCAAHC), where she served as a Commissioner from

2012-2015. Ultimately, Sharon would find herself in an intimate circle of other Afrocentric minds, seeking opportunities to support the entrepreneurial ventures of friends and the community at large.

She came ... for comradery—instead she discovered her destiny.

That night, a spark of inspiration led to the creation of Remembering Our Ancestors Synergistic Association (ROASA), Inc., and the rest, shall we say, is history. Undaunted by the task before her, Sharon simply began with one step along her purposed path, boldly placing one faithful foot in front of the other and trusting God to reveal the vision, piece by piece. Since then, the cultural enrichment organization has made an indelible mark on the Washington Metro area as a historical voice that the world has yet to hear, but soon will. True to its origin, ROASA, Inc., has created a platform rooted in connecting positive, like-minded people through the power of synergy, the hard work required to uplift a global community and a strong sense of self-knowledge by embracing their culture and heritage. Sharon dutifully walks in her calling to serve more and to inspire people of all colors to love themselves—unconditionally.

With signature programs, such as RYES, which stands for ROASA Youth Empowerment Series, pronounced "RISE", youth can benefit from educational and empowerment efforts that keep the faces of our forefathers in front of the next generation and its Ancestral Sightings program for adults, ROASA, Inc., tells stories, preserves legacies, and empowers people to become students of God and Self. In January 2016, the organization launched its masterpiece, the ROASA's Roadmap to Self-Workshop, which presents a 100-year timeline of African-American history and culture and paints a vibrant portrait of our nation—one that is diverse, inclusive, and true.

It takes a woman with a vision to stand for an entire race and those who are so often forgotten.

It takes a woman with conviction to ensure the conversation surrounding African-American history never fades, but continues to speak a legacy of faith and fortitude.

It takes a woman with heart to honor the lives of those who have come before—and after—her with her own.

It takes Sharon Parker.

"We remember all our ancestors in America and abroad"

"Hattie Parker's family will go down in history"

"Sharon Life Book"

72023364R00109

Made in the USA
Columbia, SC
10 June 2017